THE COMMITMENT PHOBE

it's not you...it's <u>him</u>

EMILY WILCOX

The Commitment Phobe: It's not you … it's him is published
under Mission Books, sectionalized division under Di Angelo
Publications INC.

MISSION BOOKS

an imprint of Di Angelo Publications.
The Commitment Phobe: It's not you … it's him. Copyright 2020
Emily Wilcox in digital and print distribution in the United States
of America.
Di Angelo Publications 4265 San Felipe St. #1100
Houston, Texas, 77027 www.diangelopublications.com
Library of congress cataloging-in-publications data

The Commitment Phobe: It's not you … it's him.
Downloadable via Kindle, iBooks and NOOK.

Library of Congress Registration Paperback

ISBN-13: 978-1-942549-56-7

1.   Non-fiction

2.   Family and Relationships ——Dating—— United States
                of America with int. Distribution.

For Dad and Steve.

Part One: The Masked Man

Part Two: Behind the Mask

Introduction

I will never forget my first love. It was 1979. His name was Adam, and he was six years old. We went to the same daycare, lived on the same street and we were inseparable. I planned our wedding on the day we met, and every subsequent playdate was utter bliss. I thought about him when I wasn't with him, looked forward to nap time and blushed every time he held my hand before crossing our neighborhood street. I loved him, and no one could take that away.

But Adam and I eventually went our separate ways, and life went on. Over the next three decades, there would be many Adams. They were not six years old, of course, and they varied in culture, profession and characteristics. But the constants that remained were the feelings I had when I was with them: love, passion and obsession. It was as if I lived in outer space, and each new man held the key to my oxygen tank. Not only could I not exist without their love but I also struggled to breathe when it was taken away. Life in outer space was painful, and I knew I would need my own key to survive.

I eventually learned unconditional love for my-self and moved to Planet Earth, where I met my husband. But prior to meeting him, I sought out answers to my many relationship questions in books, seminars, teachers, psychologists, spiri-tual gurus and even God himself. For as long as I can remember, I was obsessed with understand-ing how relationships worked.

After years of studying, I eventually became a relationship expert, offering my expansive knowledge to magazines, radio stations, advice columns, events and conventions. But what I re-alized during that time was that there was a scar-city of books that focused on men who couldn't commit. And virtually none that focused on why women (including me) kept attracting them. It became clear that my story and what I had dis-covered about commitment phobia needed to be shared. Along the way, hundreds of women came out of hiding, declaring themselves addicted to love and to the high that relationships had to of-fer. They, too, wanted to share their stories.

Being with a Commitment Phobe is like a ro-mance novel from the beginning. Flowers, affection and connection. And then reality comes crashing in, shattering our blissful little paradise, and we begin to wonder what has possibly gone wrong and how our Prince Charming has miraculously become a self-obsessed stranger. When it comes to relationships, love never quite prepares us for the Commitment Phobe.

We didn't see the pitfalls of this relationship coming. After all, this certainly wasn't the same guy we met in the beginning.

The guy we met was kind, considerate and, most of all, charming. His persistence paid off, and suddenly we were head over heels. But the utter shock toward the end left us wondering, who was this guy?

Not all men who leave relationships have issues around commitment. There are many committable men and women who decide to part ways for a myriad of reasons, and they are not part of this book. Men who can commit may share a few similarities with the Commitment Phobe, but they are by no means the same, and, as you will find out, their differences will stand out more often than not. Just like women, men also need love, affection, understanding and respect. We are equal in what we deserve and in our inherent birthrights. And even the Commitment Phobe deserves love. However, as you will understand throughout this book, it is with self-love that we can take back control of our own lives, put ourselves first and let the Commitment Phobe do the same for himself.

My goal for this book is simple: to help you see that you are worthy of all things good, making it impossible for another love affair to go south. Secondly, I want to shine a bright light on this rapidly growing phenomenon of commitment phobia. But before we can understand ourselves and this tumultuous relationship, we must first understand the man behind the mask.

You may recognize your partner, lover, boyfriend or husband throughout this book. As you read on, you will likely even think I am talking about him. But for simplicity's sake, and to avoid confusion, I will be referring to him throughout this book as the Commitment Phobe.

Part One:
The Masked Man

18   THE COMMITMENT PHOBE

CHAPTER I

The Pre-Beginning

"Kiss the hell out of me."
- Unknown

I would normally begin a story at the obvious place—the *beginning*. But this story needs to begin before the beginning. The beginning would require that I was actually alert and involved with the man in which I will be focusing on in this book. In the *beginning*, it was love. But in the *pre*-beginning, it was typically disinterest, ambivalence or maybe even avoidance. It was anything but love.

Imagine seeking out love only to sabotage it. No matter how high our degree, we cannot intellectually justify the insanity of such behavior. The Commitment Phobe fears commitment and thrives on building his ego, attempting to gain the affections of the woman he has set his sights on. Although he is seeking love, he also can't help but enjoy the coy and endearing rejections of this gal, seemingly thriving in this incessant pursuit. It's only when he catches her that things start to slowly unwind and go downhill. He never really wanted her to return his affections; he just wanted to run after her forever.

THE CHASE

In the *beginning* of this push/pull relationship, there is typically an intentional, unwavering pursuit by the man who cannot commit. He relentlessly pursues his prize (you), and his "take no prisoners" approach to getting you makes for an exciting ride (even if that ride only lasts one night). Eventually, his prey tires, and the eager charm of your insistent Prince finally wins you over. That is, until you turn to face him, unintentionally sparking his own latent fears many months later.

In the pre-beginning of this relationship, you were single, intermittently looking for love and generally minding your own business. You may even have just gotten out of another relationship with a guy you have since nicknamed "asshole." The irony, of course, is that the former asshole is appearing strikingly similar to the current guy.

Before I cover that, let's focus on what sideswiped you when you least expected it.

You were going about your life when you met this fun and interesting guy. He seemed nice and all, but really you had more interest in your 6 p.m. yoga class at that point. But he was relentless and worse, charming. While you were looking for The One and barely interested in this bozo that had inexplicably wedged himself into your so-called life, you found yourself sidetracked by his curiosity, cool demeanor and genuine interest. Suddenly, you had sleepless nights smiling at the thought of him. You were doomed, you thought. But this guy spent the majority of his time convincing you to give him a shot (even though he is a man of few words) while playing the role of the romantic love-struck Romeo. You may almost have been annoyed had you not enjoyed the attention so much.

While this guy spent the majority of his days and nights in hot pursuit of you, you perked up your interest and thought, *well, maybe*. Little did you know that in no time at all, this innocent thought would turn into a full-fledged, hell-hath-no-fury, downright nightmare.

This guy pursued you because you were initially unattainable. It was the thrill of the chase, and while you were appearing cool and confident and sometimes even attached to another man, this guy made his move. While exuding a persona of "not interested, thank you," you mystified him with your wary disinterest.

The man who can't commit sees this as a green light and makes his move with an abnormally high sense of confidence. While you have your natural guard up, appearing aloof, this non-committal man goes in for the kill and breaks that wall down, giving you the high that can only be felt when Cupid's arrow strikes. Once this cool cat cracks that wall, your addiction to love pours out, nearly drowning this guy in the process.

Subconsciously, you wonder what he possibly sees in you and why he is so insistent on choosing you, of all people. What was wrong with this guy, you wondered. But love persists, and so do you.

This mysterious man may not even have been your type. Physically, perhaps you could have done much better. But this guy had confidence and wanted to give you the world. What did looks, his clothing or his hairstyle have to do with anything, you asked yourself. You weren't materialistic, right? And somehow while you were busy sorting all of this out in your head, trying to figure out what this intense feeling was that you were starting to have and generally analyzing the hell out of things, it happened. You fell in love.

THE CHALLENGE

I think it's worthy of an honorable mention at this point that a man who can't commit enjoys going after a woman who is previously committed, married or otherwise engaged. If, when you met, you had a boyfriend, this turned him on all the more, and getting you to dump your current love was a realistic goal for this guy.

Getting you away from the other guy makes him feel powerful and at ease with himself. Subconsciously, he believes that a married woman will never suffocate or enmesh him because her energy is directed elsewhere and not at him. When it comes to intimate relationships, having the spotlight off of him feels safe.

A pastime for many of these guys is being in pursuit of a woman who is already taken because he finds her fascinating. He likes the mystery, surprise and danger of these pursuits.

They make him feel strong and give him an excuse to engage in drama outside of feeling his own feelings. This type of distraction works great for a man who can't commit until his prey leaves her bad relationship for him, generating new feelings of suffocation. The majority of these guys want to find love and have a perfect little family life or even just a committed relationship. Therefore, they would be the first to deny their own fears and limitations.

A man who can't commit is always looking for external signs and confirmation that he has found The One. When you first came along, he may have likely even believed you were The One. And several months in, when he starts to feel the relationship is losing its zest, he assumes it must mean you are *not* The One, never understanding that his inability to commit is the *real* problem.

KRISTINA'S STORY

Length of Relationship: *One year and eight months.*

Commitment Phobic Attributes: *Pseudo-confident, fearful, shutdown.*

When Kristina first met Al at a friend's wedding, she found him funny, at best. She knew she enjoyed his company during the otherwise boring reception, but at the end of the night, she said her goodbyes and went on her way.

The following day, she received a phone call from a fellow wedding attendee who informed Kristina that Al was looking for her and wanted her phone number. With a little hesitation, she obliged, and she heard from Al later that same evening.

Overlooking his quirky demeanor, Kristina began to fall for Al's charm and ability to woo her and any unsuspecting crowd. He was quite persistent and clearly knew what he wanted. The first date lasted 10 hours, and the next several days turned into weeks. Al seemed to pull down the moon for his new love, and both were in relationship bliss.

Three months after the wedding, Al began to pull away, and Kristina could feel that something just wasn't right.

However, she ignored her gut feeling and took things as they came. Al wanted to spend less and less time with Kristina, and as the months dragged on, she became unhappy, suspicious and bewildered by his strange behavior. Something wasn't right, she thought. But come hell or high water, she was going to get this relationship back on track to where it was in the *beginning*. I mean, it had only been six months so far. Much too early for his interest to wane, right?

CHAPTER 2

Defining Roles

"In most of our human relationships, we spend much of our time reassuring one another that our costumes of identity are on straight.""

- Ram Dass

Before we enter into the depths of the dramatic relationship between a Commitment Phobe and a Love Addict, we need to first identify the purpose behind the magnetic attraction and introduce the two main characters involved in this tumultuous love affair. We have all heard that it takes two to tango, and this very special duo is no exception. Both characters are equally responsible for this unhealthy relationship, and to understand one, we have to understand the other. They complete each other, attract each other and are playing out their unique roles in conjunction with their pasts.

THE COMMITMENT PHOBE

Our hero in this story is one we are all too familiar with. The Commitment Phobe wears many hats, works in various professions and comes in all races, shapes, sizes and cultures. He can cleverly disguise himself as a romantic, a gentleman, a prince or a die-hard cheerleader of Team You. Not only does this pose a difficult problem for women everywhere looking for Mr. Right but this guy is the most confused of all because the Commitment Phobe truly wants one thing—to *commit.*

This guy can sometimes appear to be the strong, silent type, and he truly wants love and acceptance as much as the next guy. But the Commitment Phobe is not the man you dreamt about as a little girl. He is neither confident nor sure of himself, but rather somewhat cocky and overly self-absorbed. He can also come across as cool and mysterious, seemingly hiding a deep secret.

The Commitment Phobe is used to burying his emotions, only bringing them to the surface in extremes. Like most of us in the world, he has issues from his past. The pain he carries is not unlike the rest of ours, but his fears can feel quite suffocating. There are many reasons for his fear of commitment, but none that have to do with his love or feelings for us.

We will obviously be discussing the Commitment Phobe in great detail throughout this book, as he is the star of the show. But first, our ingénue will be making her screen debut alongside our leading man.

THE LOVE ADDICT

Making her way down the red carpet with flashing lights and a stunning glow is our beautiful leading lady, whom I will respectfully refer to throughout this book as the Love Addict. This was a nickname coined by Pia Mellody in her book *Facing Love Addiction*. Mellody's candid books were fixtures in my late-night studies, and I am indebted to her incomparable knowledge and wisdom.

The Love Addict is not pathetic, weak or stupid. She is not the waning wallflower waiting to be asked to dance. Rather she can be spotted for her strength, honesty and secret addiction to love. She is a woman of analytical sorts, distrusting and calculating in her romantic relationships. Not altogether dissimilar to the Codependent, the Love Addict fears abandonment and will hold on to men who appear to offer her the love she lacks for herself. This willing participant, of course, is none other than our hero, the Commitment Phobe.

With a penchant for bad boys, mysterious loners and social butterflies, the Love Addict loves to love. Her need for acceptance, gratitude and affection has won her the coveted award for most "hits and misses" in relationships. Throughout this book, you may often see yourself in her, maybe rooting for her or wincing at some of her scandalous antics and bouts of insanity. You will notice she is lovable (much like you), and she is genuinely trying her best to find the right guy and have a normal, healthy relationship.

OUR COMMON FEARS

Shakti Gawain, author of *Creative Visualization,* explained it best when she wrote, "The people we are in relationship with are always a mirror, reflecting our own beliefs, and simultaneously we are mirrors, reflecting their beliefs. So... relationship is one of the most powerful tools for growth. If we look honestly at our relationships, we can see so much about how we have created them."

Hence, this dynamic duo attracts and mirrors each other over and over again, like a never-ending loop until one of them consciously and with great effort, stops this broken record. The Love Addict may even seek help to end the push/pull agony.

The Commitment Phobe and the Love Addict have very similar fears. However, they are actually the opposite of each other, making it even more obvious that these two are bound for disaster. The common fears this duo shares are intimacy and abandonment. However rare, men can also be Love Addicts, but the focus in this book is on the female addict and her willing partner in crime.

ABANDONMENT/INTIMACY

The Love Addict is very much in touch with her feelings of abandonment, meaning she is *conscious* that she fears abandonment. She knows with certainty that she does not want to be rejected in the relationship because her ability to love herself is minimal. She relies on the love of others and the Commitment Phobe (her closest ally) to be her oxygen tank.

And with a past possibly consisting of neglect, abandonment, sexual abuse, dysfunction or emotional trauma, it comes as no surprise that the Love Addict is constantly on the search for acceptance from external sources.

The pangs of some past abandonment or neglect may still lie dormant in the Love Addict, and they are constantly seeking to be healed. If you are reading this book and are still looking for The One, but keep attracting men who can't commit, you have no choice but to look backward and heal a part of you that still believes you are unworthy of love on some level. Embracing, rather than erasing, the neglected child from your past will open doors you thought were locked forever.

On the flip side, the Commitment Phobe's *subconscious* fear is abandonment, the opposite of the Love Addict. However, this guy would never think that he fears abandonment, as he mostly spends his time trying to be abandoned by his partner, avoiding the dirty work by exiting the relationship.

While the Love Addict is *conscious* of her fears surrounding abandonment, the Commitment Phobe is *conscious* that he fears intimacy. Even though she craves intimacy the most, it is what leads to the pain associated with abandonment.

The Commitment Phobe's *conscious* fear is intimacy as this is where he, too, faces possible rejection if he falls in love.

However, he is *conscious* of this fear because he thinks that intimacy will lead to enmeshment, a feeling of confinement and restriction. The actual fear is rejection, which he would never likely know on a conscious level. The Commitment Phobe also fears he could accidentally choose the wrong woman when it comes to love and, therefore, seeks perfection, which does not exist. Every time the Commitment Phobe gets too close, he backs off. When a connection is made, he weaves in and out of protection mode to avoid intimacy.

THE RESULT

Here is where it can get tricky:

The Love Addict *subconsciously* fears intimacy because it could lead to abandonment.

The Commitment Phobe *subconsciously* fears abandonment and therefore avoids intimacy.

This part is usually confusing for most because the Commitment Phobe is generally the one who exits the relationship. He leaves and hence, has successfully avoided being enmeshed and abandoned, embarking on a new pursuit of a woman he feels will never actually turn to face him and request intimacy. This new woman was you in the *beginning*.

The moral of the story is that the Love Addict and the Commitment Phobe share the same fears in the opposite direction. If you have ever wondered why the dramas, ins and outs, ups and downs and general craziness of this relationship exist, look no further. Intimacy and abandonment go hand in hand with these lovebirds. Whether emotionally or physically, one is always leaving while the other is always coming.

FEAR VS. LOVE

According to bestselling author and spiritual leader, Marianne Williamson, we operate out of two emotions: fear and love (or subcategories thereof). Fear can manifest as jealousy, anger, worry, distrust, lying or manipulation, to name a few. Love manifests as joy, empathy, compassion, kindness, generosity, peace, calm and understanding.

At any given time, both of our main characters function out of fear rather than love, often without ever realizing and mistaking love for lust. For the Love Addict, her fears manifest as worry of abandonment. If she were functioning through love, she would easily see that if her partner rejects her, that is his issue. The Commitment Phobe's fears result in him running away. When he is operating through love, he only sees his partner and himself as human with an undeniable connection.

Our fear is housed by the ego, which is fragile and leaves us susceptible to pain brought on by the words, judgments and complaints of our partners, families and peers. Our ego needs to feel important. Our *real* self knows we are already beyond important and perfectly whole. When we treat our ego as something real, it will fight for positioning and win every time.

THE ORIGIN OF FEAR

Fundamentally, fear protects us from physical danger. Since the beginning of humankind, we have slowly and unintentionally used fear to protect ourselves from emotional pain. The hard part is learning to greet our fear, knowing it is intended for the purpose of protection from danger.

Success does not happen in the absence of fear because completely expelling fear from our lives is an impossible task. But when it comes to relationships, fear should not take a front seat. When it does, both parties, if healthy, will openly discuss these fears and help each other move forward. Relationships don't have problems, people do, and our fears have nothing to do with our partners. Rather, fear is a past conditioning that holds steadfast until confronted. With introspection and determination, we can move through our fears consciously and forcefully, as opposed to fruitlessly waiting for them to dissipate on their own.

SOPHIA'S STORY

Length of Relationship: *One year and nine months.*

Commitment Phobic Attributes: *Fear, escapism,*

indecision.

Sophia was a product of divorce. Her father moved out early on and left her with her mother and sister. He visited a few times a month but was not very present and even less affectionate. More than anything, Sophia wanted her father to hug and love her. He just didn't know how. Sophia spent much of her adult life seeking attention from the men around her, never quite realizing that she was attempting to find love from any outside source who seemed to offer it to her.

Eventually, Sophia met Blaine. He was everything and more, and she felt her search for The One had finally come to an end. Blaine had a pretty typical childhood. His father was a workaholic, and his mother smothered Blaine with attention, often making him the sole provider of her love and affection. She was dependent on him, and that was overwhelming for Blaine at such a young age. On top of that, he missed his father, who was away all of the time.

When these two lovebirds began their subconscious dance, they were drawn to each other like magnets. Blaine showered Sophia with attention, and he was initially in his comfort zone.

But Blaine eventually pulled away after feeling suffocated once Sophia accepted his advances. When he finally exited the relationship, he created a massive fight and left. When he changed his mind a few weeks later and came back around, Sophia was waiting for him, and they started their love affair all over again, repeating all of the steps from the *beginning* to the end at lightning-fast speed.

CHAPTER 3

The Beginning: Your Knight in Shining Armor

"Infatuation is not quite the same thing as love; it's more like love's shady second cousin who's always borrowing money and can't hold down a job."
- Elizabeth Gilbert,
  Committed: A Skeptic Makes Peace with Marriage

At the blissful early stage, you (the Love Addict) sincerely believe that your relationship is happy, healthy and thriving. Planning a future and canoodling in bed are your favorite pastimes, and you are falling head over heels for your knight in shining armor. It turns out that the man in the *beginning* is not the man in the end. They are worlds apart, and no one could have seen it coming.

The man from the pre-beginning who persisted and won you over against your better judgment is now a full-fledged Facebook-official boyfriend (if he was brave enough to move past *that* fear).

He's amazing, you're amazing and you declare to your friends and family that you are finally in love, and it was well worth the wait after kissing all those frogs. Even more, you remain convinced and thankful for how you didn't let this guy go based on materialistic matters or social status. What a foolish move that would have been, you tell yourself. The Universe must have really wanted you to be with this guy!

The Commitment Phobe is everything you ever wanted and more. If you were unlucky with the recipe of love before, this guy certainly has the missing ingredient.

WOLF IN SHEEP'S CLOTHING

Perhaps his method of operation to win over your affections was writing adorable little love notes and expressing his joy that he finally has you in his arms. Maybe it's sending flowers when you least expected it. A favorite is the silly, fun text messages you would receive throughout your boring, predictable workday.

The Commitment Phobe is great at acting the part of Mr. Right. But the truth is that the *real* Mr. Right would never appear so strange and mysterious, creepily deliberate or, in truth, desperate. Mr. Right acts much more normal than this guy. It doesn't matter that the Commitment Phobe is a little different. After all, that is part of his charm and allure. This current Mr. Right is right for *you*, and that's all that matters...until it isn't.

THE BAD BOY

Let's just be honest. There was a time when the nice guy finished last, and attention from some nerd at the bar made us roll our eyes and giggle with our friends over his stupid Hawaiian-themed shirt. We wanted a tough guy, one who played it cool and overcompensated for his super low self-image. Surely this guy had the balls to pull off a Hawaiian-flowered shirt, right?

Often, but not always, the Love Addict is attracted to the bad boy because he appears mysterious and cool. And if she can get this guy to love her, then she would *really* feel worthy.

DO NOT DISTURB

It didn't even matter that he seemed a bit emotionally unavailable. You figured he would eventually open up and become more intimate. After all, he was your soul mate!

The sex was so incredible that it would eventually turn into *making love*, right? No one could deny this magical, magnetic connection. Surely, not even the Commitment Phobe would argue about the physical fireworks that went off when the two of you were lost in the sheets. You may have even started calling in sick just so you could spend more time lying in bed from long, cosmic romp sessions, after which you were physically numb and emotionally high. It didn't matter nor occur to you that a real man would nudge you toward being responsible and maintaining your integrity by showing up to work. I mean, this was love!

You spent hours staring at the stars with this man, hoping and dreaming that what you felt was the real deal, and that one day, you two would ride off into the sunset and be the perfect example of true love. There would be romance novels written in your honor. But after the first several months, things slowly start to change, and your Prince Charming begins to reveal a different face. This does not yet cause a great deal of concern for you because it is very slight and hardly noticeable. Unless, of course, you're looking. Forget about the fact that your family feels this train is moving much too fast, or that you have almost dropped all of your friends so that you can cuddle on the couch and watch *Three's Company* reruns while playing hooky from your job. You were in love and thoroughly convinced that all women drop their friends for a man during the Honeymoon Phase. And while there may be some truth to this, the Commitment Phobe somehow takes it to a whole other level.

Along with the amazing sex, long phone calls and shared ideas on the future, the *beginning* of the relationship with a Commitment Phobe is actually much more like a physical magnet pulling two people together to recreate the past. This is why many Love Addicts explain the connection as indescribably intense. All signposts begin to make sense when we come to understand that we reap what we sow, live what we know and map out a future based exactly on our past.

TOO FAST, TOO SOON

The Love Addict explains herself well at this stage, telling her friends and family, "I know it's all happening very fast, but it feels so right!" And the Commitment Phobe is so excited about this new love affair that he can barely contain himself. After all, pursuing you (the Love Addict) really made him realize that you must be The One! These crazy feelings must be a sign from the heavens above because they couldn't *possibly* be driven by the thrill of playing hard-to-get. When he is talking about marriage, kids, moving in and meeting the family (all within the first month!), you should consider these red flags because *this* Honeymoon Phase won't last long.

When it comes to a relationship with the Commitment Phobe, the Love Addict expresses (either openly or silently) how amazing it was in the *beginning*. The *beginning* becomes an insidious mantra, as she prays for her time machine to take her back to the man she fell in love with. The only problem is that just as Michael J. Fox has moved on with his acting career, so has the Commitment Phobe.

RELATIONSHIP LENGTH

The length of this relationship varies based on age, culture and individual characteristics. For example, in many countries, cheating is considered forgivable and not unusual, giving those relationships a considerably longer shelf life than their counterparts in other cultures who see infidelity and disrespect as grounds for immediate termination.

Typically, around six to nine months into a relationship with the Commitment Phobe, most Love Addicts begin to sense that something just doesn't feel right. At one and a half years, there are full-blown insecurities on both parts, if they have not sprung up earlier. The majority of Commitment Phobes seldom surpass the *two-year* time frame without taking a "break." When they do, it is usually at the cost of the relationship's health due to disloyalty, affairs or compulsive lying. Divorced Commitment Phobes typically fall under this category.

If this relationship does last beyond the typical two-year mark, it is a slippery slope and an utter war zone at times. Some Commitment Phobes have had many short relationships, while others may have had none. The quantity of past girlfriends is not a distinguishing characteristic. The difference is that the Commitment Phobe will not have come out of a healthy, five-year committed relationship, departing due to simple differences or growing apart.

This relationship rarely lasts more than two years without issues, separations, fighting, shutting down or cheating. After a time, the Love Addict can lose perspective because she is constantly thinking about the man she met in the *beginning*, making her forget that the first few years are supposed to be the *best* years, not the *worst*.

THREE MONTHS OF BLISS

No matter how long this relationship lasts, the

first three months are the most telling. During this time with a Commitment Phobe, life as you know it is officially over. You have closed all of your dating site profiles, dropped your backups, changed your Facebook status and generally considered yourself taken. And boy, were you ever taken. The deep feelings and big plans he shares with you in the *beginning* can last anywhere between a few days and several months.

During these first few pivotal months, the Commitment Phobe is working his magic and has tricks up his sleeve that would put Casanova to shame. Whether or not he is aware of his espionage is dependent on his individual "inner marker," which will be discussed at length in a later chapter.

The Commitment Phobe may not realize that the Honeymoon Phase naturally comes to an end, causing the realwork to begin. Since he is too self-involved to do any work on this relationship, things begin to fall by the wayside. When you show your flaws, he gets scared.

STACEY'S STORY

Length of Relationship: *One year and one month.*

Commitment Phobic Attributes: *Charming,*

distant, cheating.

Stacey and Scott spent every day together. They were like Bonnie and Clyde, Fred and Ginger or Sonny and Cher. They equally avoided their friends and family. Even work was coming in second. He was totally enamored, and she was a smitten kitten.

On the weekends, they would drive up to his dad's empty cabin and fish for salmon, which Stacey found new and exciting. Every event was "us" and "we," while each day became a new dream. The *beginning* was everything Stacey could have wanted, but the relationship eventually deteriorated.

Nine months into this love affair, Scott grew distant and wanted space. Under the radar, he started hanging out with his ex-girlfriend, found a few new female friends and was spending much more time with the guys. The man she knew in the *beginning* stole her heart, and she continued to search for him in a withdrawn, shell of a person who rarely slept by her side anymore.

CHAPTER 4

Empty Promises

"In any relationship in which two people become one, the end result is two half people."

- Wayne Dyer

By this time, the Commitment Phobe has loaded up your emotional calendar with suggestions of children, family and a future filled with adventure and travel. Playing house can be this guy's most fulfilling pastime. After all, what the Commitment Phobe typically wants more than anything is to commit! He may work tirelessly to keep you holding on to this relationship while he begins to wander in and out of it. But he can't let you go, so he comes bearing gifts and convincing words filled with promise—a representation of who he wishes he could be.

THE "FAMILY" MAN

This man can sometimes be the first to tell

you that he wants to fall in love, get married and start a family. But, buyer beware: actions speak louder than words.

Sure, this guy likes spending a lot of time with you, but he may be the first to admit that he doesn't know what real love is. If you need your grandma's intuition, a team of psychics, a therapist, your angel guides and a coin toss to figure out if this guy loves you, this may be a sign you are dancing dangerously too close to a Commitment Phobe.

This guy was even adamant that he wanted children just as much as you did. While you spent your childhood nursing baby-wets-a-lot, he has virtually convinced you that he spent his adolescent years doing the same thing. But lo and behold, as it turns out, your gleaming father-to-be ended up changing his mind, usually somewhere during the first twelve months of this push/pull relationship.

Your dreams of buying your kid an Easy-Bake Oven and arguing over which preschool to send him or her to have been abruptly shattered when the Commitment Phobe finally confesses he does not want children, at least not anytime soon. After all, the relationship has problems now, and he doesn't think it's wise to discuss such important issues within a damaged union (forget about the fact that he caused the damage). He begins to insist that fixing the relationship before moving further is what is best for everyone.

This is the Commitment Phobe's way of buying time and delaying further commitment. While he talks about the relationship needing work, he does nothing to actually work on it.

THE PROMISE RING

It is unusual for the Commitment Phobe to catch his anxiety-ridden breath long enough to hit the nearest jeweler and buy a faux diamond ring to profess his unending commitment to the girl of his dreams. (That's you, for now.) You have been persistent in your complaints regarding his non-committal ways, and he feels tremendous pressure to act quickly before he loses you completely. So, he comes up with the most romantic antic since Romeo's suicide: the promise ring.

I love hearing about the promise ring from my clients because it reminds me of that scene in *The Breakfast Club* when Ally Sheedy pulls Emilio Estevez's wrestling patch from his letterman jacket, and they exchange that eye-to-eye romantic glare that says, *you're mine forever because I now have your stupid patch*.

I have had grown adult women sit in my office and flash their drugstore promise rings as if it were the greatest thing on Earth. "Look, he is promising to get me an engagement ring!" A ring to promise another ring? An intelligent woman can sometimes lose all objectivity when involved with a Commitment Phobe. It all becomes too ridiculous when you start using your whole brain to analyze this. You have already begun the steady decline into the Commitment Phobe's insane world of illusion and deceit, so you truly believe in this magical ring. This is *his* promise to eventually promise you that he might eventually promise to give you a real ring, the kind that you can actually pawn later. I know what you're thinking: *He* is the one who wanted to marry *me*,...and he likely even did...until his fear took over.

WORDPLAY

Next to Japanese, Croatian and Pig Latin, the Commitment Phobe has his own language. He likes to use words that are officially in the dictionary and then create sentences that manipulate the Love Addict's feelings of safety and hope. An example of this may be: "Someday, maybe we will be together down the road permanently one day in the future, possibly." He somehow knows we will instantly take our favorite words (together, permanently and future), leaving the others behind like unwanted trash. The Love Addict is like Inspector Gadget: specifically looking for signs, signals and clues that there is a highlighted map to the future, leading to that one big happy family. But this is a clue—a huge clue—that this guy is full of hot air and should get jail time for his malicious use of *Merriam-Webster's Dictionary*. But once we have a grip on that map, it can take the "jaws of life" to yank that thing from our tiny little paws. The idea of forever sends chills down his spine, and the Commitment Phobe can rarely utter "I want to spend my life with you" without choking on his words or having several cocktails.

THE FUTURE'S SO BRIGHT, I GOTTA WEAR SHADES

Ah, the future. Full of promise, joy, hope...and commitment. Things always seem glorious in the future with the Commitment Phobe. No matter how bad the present, it never ceases to amaze me how much effort, energy and work we place on the future and, oh, how the Commitment Phobe loves to feed us hope for the future. He knows exactly what our little ears need to hear to stay in this relationship.

Everything with the Commitment Phobe always seems to be "one day." Later on in the relationship, we are disappointed that we never even stopped to think about how miserable the situation really was. But that's okay...we have the future! Only it's not full of babies, white picket fences, adventure and love. It turns out that *this* future ends up in pain, heartbreak, chronic confusion and mind-numbing anger.

You rest assured that the best is yet to come because soon you will be looking back with fond memories at the good old days of empty promises. What happens next turns out to be more shocking than being duped by a stupid, little gumball machine promise ring.

HEATHER'S STORY

Length of Relationship: *Two years.*

Commitment Phobic Attributes: *Wordplay, indecisiveness, fear.*

When Heather first met Tom, he was overly insistent on marriage and family, almost to the degree that Heather was feeling a bit suffocated and perplexed.

"He was the one who brought up marriage and kids. I was actually confused because it was so early in the dating process!" Heather proclaimed during one of our sessions.

Heather's confusion soon turned into understanding when she realized Tom actually did want these things in the *beginning*. It was his fears and indecision that kept him from following through. In a private session with Tom, he was open enough to admit that he was always looking for the better option when it came to love. He was worried that he may end up settling for Heather, and that there may be someone better around the next corner.

This is pretty typical thinking for a Commitment Phobe. Although Tom had self-reflection and introspection, he was resistant to change. Heather found the strength to leave Tom and eventually struck up quite a serious love relationship with herself, followed quickly by a committed and confident new man.

CHAPTER 5

The Switch

"Where there is no struggle, there is no strength."
- Oprah Winfrey

After the flowers have stopped arriving, the phone has stopped ringing and the Honeymoon Phase has come to an abrupt end, something unexpected happens. But before I get into that pivotal turning point, let's recap.

In the *beginning,* the relationship with the Commitment Phobe was like a breath of fresh air. He was everything you ever wanted: attentive, understanding, present and loving. Most of all, *he* pursued *you* because in the pre-beginning, you may not have even been very interested in this guy. Certainly not as much as he was in you. In fact, many of you couldn't care less if he disappeared into the great abyss. As he kept up his diligent pursuit, you gave in. Things were amazing...for a while.

THE TURNAROUND

As fast as you could say supercalifragilisticex-pialidocious, the tables were turned, and you found yourself in hot pursuit of the man that spent weeks or even months trying to get you to even give him a second look. For every two steps forward, he seemed to take five steps back. The man who was once pursuing you like you were his last meal has surprisingly shifted gears, heading in a direction that didn't include you.

Where once he was the hunter and you were the prey, now the roles are reversed. This crazy turn of events has you stunned and unable to comprehend your own name. "How did this happen?" you ask yourself with understandable anger and irritation. The man who once pulled the world out of his pocket and handed it to you on a silver platter has now turned his back on you.

Suddenly, you feel needy and desperate, as your Prince Charming has turned into the uninterested, elusive party. There was a time when this guy would have killed tigers in your honor, and now he can barely take his eyes off of the television long enough to say *hello* when you walk in the door. Meanwhile, you spend your time wondering what went wrong. Why is the relationship in shambles, and where is the guy from the *beginning*?

After the switch occurs, all you can think about is the relationship and how to keep it going. You become a little too obsessed with this guy. You begin to wonder if it's *you*, and you start to do everything you can to overextend yourself in the relationship. You become the perfect partner, giving him everything you think a man wants. Your lingerie drawer is full from your failed attempts at intimacy, your job is playing second fiddle to your once storybook romance and you can barely drag him off his emotional couch to snag a little affection. His capacity for emotional introspection has become likened to Roger Rabbit. Who was this guy? You convince yourself that the man in the *beginning* was real and that this new guy is some sort of impostor who has temporarily invaded his brain.

PUSH/PULL

In this relationship, one person is always pushing, and the other is always pulling. This kind of interaction is a sure survival method for one or both of these offenders. The Commitment Phobe is in a fearful state regarding commitment, and the Love Addict is in a state of needing him to love her as both parties fear intimacy and abandonment.

Typically, several months to a year into the relationship is when the pull happens for the Commitment Phobe. He may emotionally shut down after a lovely weekend or simply decide to disappear for a few days altogether. Each time the Commitment Phobe pulls away, the longer he takes to stretch his arms and return to you. For the Love Addict, these actions threaten to sabotage her waning relationship. Pulling away when he gets close, the Commitment Phobe's fear of intimacy can wreak havoc on the Love Addict's need for connection. Just when everything was going great, this guy gets scared that the closeness may be too much for him to handle. He may pull away for a day or for weeks, but as the relationship continues, each time he clocks out, it's for a longer period of time than the last. Breaking up and making up are part of his dysfunctional indecisiveness.

When the Commitment Phobe pulls away, it can be the most damaging of techniques for the Love Addict because her fears of pending abandonment are triggered. She would almost rather he cause a fight. At least he would be showing her *some* attention.

The push/pull starts off slowly and picks up speed. As the relationship continues, it becomes a regular occurrence. One is always running away while the other is always chasing, rarely coming face-to-face with each other. When they stop to connect in between chases is when the passion ignites, and the world stands still again. The love they feel in these fleeting moments is what keeps the relationship alive. Both parties believe that this attraction they continue to feel is why they are so deeply connected. But it's not long before the good times fade, and the routine begins all over again.

The pulling away by the Commitment Phobe almost always happens when things seem to be going exceptionally well, usually right after that interim of deep connection. This occurs because the intimacy is getting much too intense for the Commitment Phobe, who may even start a fight, seemingly out of nowhere, to get the push/pull started once again. This is the most confusing aspect of the dance for the Love Addict, who is blindsided by this behavior because, in her mind, everything was going well and looking like the *beginning* again!

Let's not confuse the Commitment Phobe's extreme avoidance techniques with a committable man who rightfully needs his space. In *Men Are from Mars, Women Are from Venus*, acclaimed author John Gray points out that "a man automatically alternates between needing intimacy and autonomy." While this is certainly the case with a healthy man, the Commitment Phobe leans much too often toward autonomy and doesn't come back until compelled by fear or a lasso. Space is good within any relationship, but we aren't talking about just *any* relationship.

If the pusher and puller can realize what is actually going on here (two adults perpetuating old fears), then they may be able to work on the relationship together with some professional outside help. This approach can bring up a lot of deep-seated emotional wounds for the Commitment Phobe, who is not typically fond of sorting through his feelings the way the Love Addict is.

HIGHS AND LOWS

For this kind of couple, the highs are very high,

and the lows are very low. The Love Addict lives for the highs, waiting patiently for them after each low. But the high turns into a bad omen because the Commitment Phobe shuts down right afterward. Things between this duo become consistently *inconsistent.* Each time the relationship is amazing again, the Love Addict convinces herself that her knight is back, and all is well in the world. No matter how many times he comes and goes emotionally, she hopes against hope that *this* time it will stick.

WALKING ON EGGSHELLS

Worried that any mention of the word *relationship* or even *hello* might drive the Commitment Phobe into a fear frenzy, the Love Addict walks on eggshells and waits for things to diffuse and get good again. She doesn't want to scare him away, so she suddenly acts like the cool, disinterested party, making him believe that she doesn't need him at all. The truth is her feelings do scare him, but the Love Addict may avoid all communication and affection to keep her guy around a little longer. Ironically, men love to be needed, and a healthy committable man would walk away from such aloofness and mystery. We will discuss this phenomenon later on.

REMINISCING

After hell freezes over and pigs fly, you spend the remainder of the relationship desperately trying to convince yourself that it will eventually go back to what it was like in the *beginning*. You even recreate certain events that struck the love chord long ago.

With your new Victoria's Secret credit card in hand, you look to spice things up and get this party going once again. But you are suddenly in a relationship with an unemotional zombie, and you are playing the part of the bright and cheery dancing queen, smiling and trying to keep this ship from sinking. Not only are you at a loss for words, sex and sympathy but also this new dynamic has left you dumbfounded.

What happened to the man from the *beginning*? Here is the thing: this guy does not have amnesia. The Commitment Phobe is well aware of what it was like in the *beginning*. Unlike you, however, he is not intent on getting that back. He is happily unhappy in his new role as the aloof, dégagé and unresponsive party. But the fact remains that this is not the man you knew in the *beginning*. That guy was amazing, understanding, dedicated, attentive and easy to talk to. He was everything you dreamed your perfect man would be. He loved you for you, and you loved him for him. Nothing could have been more perfect. So, when the tables turn, no one is more surprised than you.

KELLY'S STORY

Length of Relationship: *One year and six months.*

Commitment Phobic Attributes: *Persistent, alcoholic, irresponsible.*

It was at the company Christmas party that Kelly met her beau. Muhammad was charming, sweet, confident and, most of all, she connected with him on a deeper level than any of her past boyfriends.

Muhammad pursued Kelly, and she gave in after just a few short days. But nine months into the relationship, things took a dramatic turn, and Kelly suddenly became the chaser while Muhammad was determined not to be caught.

In her darkest moments, Kelly's mind would wander to what possibly could have gone so terribly wrong. *How did this happen?* she wondered. *He was the one who came after me*, she thought. *Did he change his mind? Has he lost interest?* But what Kelly didn't know was that this sudden change had nothing to do with anything she did, didn't do or could have done. She was on the other side now, and there was no going back.

CHAPTER 6
The Beginning of the End

"The ego mind both professes its desire for love and does everything possible to repel it, or if it gets here anyway, to sabotage it.'"
 - Marianne Williamson, Interview with
Psychology Today

Because the real problems usually begin between six months and two years into the relationship, this is around the time when the first actual breakup occurs. Both the Commitment Phobe and the Love Addict's self-fulfilling prophecies make them equally responsible for the beginning of the end.

Relationships are complicated enough without the added pressure of trying to always second guess what the Commitment Phobe will do at any given moment. But it's the never-ending back and forth swing stance that wreaks havoc just when the Love Addict least expects it. The Love Addict can begin to feel when the end is coming, instinctively knowing that something just isn't right, and impending doom is knocking at the door.

At this point, the Commitment Phobe starts to shut down, and getting him to open up about what is going on inside is like pulling teeth. Psychic hotlines and psychotherapists depend on this man being closed off for the betterment of their businesses and the Love Addict's insistence on uncovering the truth. The Love Addict can prod, push, yell and pull, but this guy is unmovable, and such nagging is a surefire way to create unwanted angst, causing her to eventually be marked as the crazy one. The fairy tale of the perfect match eventually turns into a relationship that is full of fluctuating passion, endless turmoil, destructive drama and a lot of pushing and pulling.

After the Honeymoon Phase has trickled down to a barely crafted, makeshift partnership, the Love Addict works even harder at getting the Commitment Phobe to open up and tell her what he is feeling. No matter how fruitless her past failed attempts, trying to get back to the *beginning* of this relationship is always her goal, and the waning communication on the other end can often make this feel like an impossible task. But just when she thinks it couldn't get any worse, it does.

LOSS OF AFFECTION

As things start winding down, waiting around for this guy to show affection can be less fun than a root canal.

When the going gets tough, you can literally feel the Commitment Phobe get going. You find yourself praying he will reach out for your hand and whisper he loves you.

When it doesn't happen, you settle for the crumbs of him patting you on the leg with a disgruntled yawn. In retrospect, this guy certainly wasn't the most affectionate person in the world. The times he held your hand, rubbed your back or cuddled with you in bed were few and far between. But nowadays, you are lucky if you accidentally bump into him in the hallway.

The Commitment Phobe's sudden lack of affection is a glaring red flag. When a behavior suddenly ends, and there is no sign of its triumphant return, it is time to gather some objectivity. The fleeting feelings of a Commitment Phobe have absolutely nothing to do with you and everything to do with his own fears, insecurities and lack of emotional strength.

GOODBYE, SEX

Practically begging for sex can supply loads of enjoyment for you (the Love Addict)! If you constantly find yourself inching toward him in bed while he drifts away into a dreamless sleep, this could be a sign of things to come. A satisfying relationship requires physical intimacy on both ends. If the Commitment Phobe no longer has the desire to offer that connection, this may not necessarily be a sign of infidelity. It can also be his way of silently removing himself from the confines of the relationship.

It's not as if the Commitment Phobe suddenly does not want to have sex. He just doesn't want to have sex with *you* because it is causing him unease. This is certainly not a reflection on anything you did wrong or could have done differently. Even your visits to the sex expert or lingerie store are proving to be futile. The Commitment Phobe seems disinterested in you no matter what you do. While once vehemently against it, you may even score some porn to bring that groove back. It's starting to feel like nothing can drag his affections in your direction.

Making love in the back of his car, a little naughty fun at the movie theater and other tasteful endeavors have now become distant memories. You suddenly find yourself longing for the sex life that once made you feel so alive. Now, on a good day, you will settle for jerking him off while he is half asleep and convincing yourself that you just made love.

JEALOUSY

The Love Addict often spends time dreading the thought of the Commitment Phobe being with another woman. She may even obsess on his wavering ways and look for clues that he has a wandering eye. And while he may, in fact, be wandering, the Love Addict needs to look at her own feelings of jealousy and how they are negatively affecting the partnership. Short of exiting the relationship, there is nothing the Love Addict can do to stop the Commitment Phobe from looking elsewhere or engaging in undesirable behavior with other women. She has to clean up her own side of the street and question where this jealousy is coming from and why she fears the Commitment Phobe will hurt her.

Rarely does this push/pull relationship escape the grips of jealousy on both ends. Of course, the ultimate goal is to be with someone who doesn't have a crippling fear of losing his or her partner and vice versa. Commitment Phobes and Love Addicts alike tend to confuse jealousy with love. In the absence of jealousy there is trust, which is needed for the ultimate survival of any healthy relationship. Trust is always at the core. So, it should come as no surprise that jealousy and fear of abandonment go hand in hand. Jealousy and love are not related. In fact, they have never even met.

SHALLOW HAL

In general, women want a man who is truthful, shares his innermost thoughts and generally has a good amount of depth. I mean, no woman wants a blubbering crybaby on her hands, but a little tear never hurt anyone, right? The problem is that the Commitment Phobe often has the depth of a puddle. When he's not blubbering about losing you or pouring out his heart in desperation, he is scarcely sharing his childhood memories and talking about his feelings (like he may have in the *beginning*).

Even then, he usually fell short of any real emotional depth. The Commitment Phobe can fluctuate between extremes, from anger and depression to happiness and elation. Balance is rarely a part of his emotional repertoire.

It is very difficult for the Commitment Phobe to show his feelings mostly because he keeps them hidden. He fears that if he begins to open up, his emotional threshold could crack, and he would be too overwhelmed by the intense emotions he has stuffed down for so long. These unmet feelings come from his past and childhood. Since these feelings ranging from neglect to abandonment to abuse have never been resolved, they lie dormant until awakened by the Love Addict.

ON HIS TERMS

At a certain point in this push/pull relationship, the Love Addict loses her sense of control, almost unwillingly. Her idea of a date night might be dinner at her favorite Italian place, followed by a romantic comedy and ice cream. The only problem is, she is no longer planning the dates. He is calling all the shots: when to hang out, call, text, hold hands or say, "I love you." The Commitment Phobe is *committing* to calling all the shots. Besides, the Love Addict dare not appear needy or vulnerable by reaching out or having an idea of her own. What if she were rejected?

The Commitment Phobe will also often have a hard time labeling the love affair and may avoid frightening words such as *girlfriend*, *boyfriend* or *relationship*. Living on someone else's terms slowly steals the Love Addict's identity. And just when she has had enough and wants to move on, he pulls a rabbit out of his indecisive hat. This emotional rollercoaster becomes like an unwanted parasite, and the Commitment Phobe knows just what to say to keep the Love Addict hanging on, and he offers just enough to keep her wanting more.

COMMUNICATION BREAKDOWN

At this point in the relationship, our Prince Charming has become reclusive and secretive, barely communicating at all. However, looking back, the communication from this mystery man in the *beginning* was never really up to snuff. However, due to the early onset of magnetic impulsive chemistry, the Love Addict was under the impression that this was a good substitute for communication. In retrospect, the Commitment Phobe was a man of few words from the get-go.

Communication can make or break a relationship.

Granted, men are not prone to talk about their feelings in quite the same way that women are. However, a committable man will not shut down at the first sign of a problem. The Commitment Phobe will often turn a blind eye whenever issues within the relationship arise. If the communication is lost, everything else will fall by the wayside, leaving you wondering if the two of you ever spoke the same language.

MICHELLE'S STORY

Length of Relationship: *One year and nine months.*

Commitment Phobic Attributes: *Loss of physical intimacy, self-absorbed, in and out.*

Nine months into their relationship, Zach slowly began to pull away from Michelle sexually. His once advanced libido had turned into a commercial for Viagra, and Michelle was feeling unattractive and underappreciated. It seemed as if Zach pulled even further away with each physical advance that Michelle made. She started to question their connection, creating more confusion and frustration.

Having a date night planned with Zach for 8 o'clock one evening, Michelle spent that Saturday afternoon getting her hair and nails done, shopping for some sexy red lingerie and generally preparing for the big event. She was determined to reignite that spark and bring her Romeo back home to Verona.

Right at 8 p.m., the stage was set: mushroom crepes with truffle sauce, strawberry salad with goat cheese and chocolate fondue to end the evening. She was wearing a simple dress that, given the opportunity, would happily reveal her secret weapon.

She had been feeling desperate to get Zach excited about her again and could hardly wait for the evening to begin.

By 8:30 p.m., Michelle was getting worried. She received a text and stopped for a moment to silently pray he was just running late from work again. She picked up her phone and read: Still in a meeting. *Sorry, babe. Rain check?*

A few months later, Zach broke up with Michelle. She was devastated, even though there was not much left of Zach to lose. She mourned the man he was in the *beginning*. Zach did everything he could to make sure Michelle didn't move on in case he changed his mind down the road. But Michelle stayed strong and didn't allow herself to remain friends, ignoring his calls and attempts to keep his foot in the door. When he finally begged her to come back, Michelle had already moved on.

CHAPTER 7

Waiting, Wondering, Hoping

"How much of human life is lost in waiting!"
  - Ralph Waldo Emerson, "Prudence," Essays

The Commitment Phobe is officially not following your lead as you attempt to get this relationship back on track. Your one-woman show is making you anxious and concerned, to say the least. *If he could just see how good we have it,* you tell yourself, *everything would be perfect.*

But alas, all of your attempts have fallen short, and while you still pull some tricks out of the old hat here and there, you are now living on a wing and a prayer. You wait, wonder and hope that the Commitment Phobe wakes up one day and realizes he is missing out on the best thing that ever happened to him.

It is important to accept that this once loving

Romeo is not saving the best of himself for last. He is not hiding a bag of tricks for later on to surprise you with. He is literally *showing you who he is.* Dreaming he were different is a long road to disappointment. Without introspection, acknowledgment and awareness, the Commitment Phobe is stuck in his own version of reality that includes *not seeking to change.*

WAITING

Hanging on for the Commitment Phobe to express love, loyalty and respect is like having a cool car with only the back wheels and wishing it had the additional two wheels it needed to be perfect. But no, you don't give up! Not *you*! You can wait this thing out! You are going to lift the front of that damn car with all of your might and attempt to hold it there because you are convinced that the man you met in the *beginning* will eventually wake up, smell the coffee and replace those tires to make the car run, rolling off into relationship bliss. If only this guy had two tires to offer!

Too often the Love Addict leaves the fate of her future in the hands of the Commitment Phobe, waiting for him to decide if he wants to be with her or not. This relinquishing of power is a distinguishing sign that the relationship has taken on a whole new meaning.

WONDERING

While you are waiting for something, anything, to magically change (mostly him because you are totally normal for staying in this relationship), you wonder what will become of your future. If you stay with the Commitment Phobe, will you ever be happy? How will you learn to trust him again? Will he eventually open up? Can it just go back to the way it was in the *beginning*?

Remember, this guy showered you with lots of promises (you still can't get over that ring) and said many things that gave you hope and encouragement that this relationship was heading somewhere. These past statements he made run rampant through your mind. In fact, recalling his previous expressions of love is what keeps you hanging on at this point. You aren't living for the current mess that the relationship has become; you are surviving on the fumes that were once a beautiful Mercedes. These thoughts of the past and what he used to say keep you going. They get you to work in the morning, keep up your appetite and allow you to generally survive the day. And you are not going to let those pesky "negative" aspects like him pulling away from you for days on end get you down. You even begin to wonder why he is acting so strange after you have been giving him all the space in the world and have been the most understanding partner. You wonder why he just can't see how good he has it! Unfortunately, he just isn't looking at you enough. On top of the fact that his fears cannot be triggered or allayed based upon your actions. This issue is in *him*.

As time ticks by more slowly than a celebrity murder trial, you become so accustomed to living on fumes and dog scraps that eventually this is all you need and require. Your standards have become so low that any little kiss on the cheek, brush of the shoulder or sentence that contains the word "love" (even if it's I love bacon) seems to be enough to get you through the week. Until, of course, it isn't. And, at that point, it won't matter because you have become so skilled at sniffing out dog scraps! So much so that you even start mistaking scraps for things like getting a phone call returned. Even if it is five days later,...*and* he hung up on the machine. This was your version of love now, and no one can take that away.

HOPING

Nothing says foolishness like a woman doing

somersaults and circus tricks to get a man to notice how lucky he is to have her. But oftentimes, the Love Addict will spin her wheels trying to get the Commitment Phobe to take notice of how amazing she is. This is about as silly as putting on a fifth-grade talent show, dressing up in a tutu and dancing circles around him.

We, the Love Addicts, can also while away the hours just hoping that this guy will grow out of his freewheeling pre-pubescent party boy ways. If he acts like an overgrown, irresponsible child, do not wait around for him to change. A boy will not become a man through our instruction and perseverance. He will only grow up on his own time, and usually, trial and error will be the route that he finds his responsibility and prominent manhood. And that simply won't happen when we are continually there to clean up his mess.

We should not be in a relationship hoping that one day we will be appreciated for our wonderfully unique qualities. When we start to play into a role of what we think he wants as opposed to being our truthful, humanly flawed and vulnerable selves, we end up sacrificing our integrity and losing who we are in the process. If he doesn't see us as amazing, incredible and worthy now, he won't wake up one day and see the light. Unless, of course, we permanently drop him like a bad habit, forcing him to feel the loss. Even then, change is unlikely.

Spending our time trying to figure out what is going on in his mind seems to be a hobby we never intended on taking up. And worse, this new hobby has taken precedence over all the others... like being happy...and smiling.

While we hope that things will turn out in our favor (all he has to do is remember the man he was in the *beginning* and start acting like him), we have become Mary Sunshine to his face and Debbie Downer behind his back. We have officially developed our own personal debilitating version of *the woman with two faces*. The Commitment Phobe has us in a tailspin, and what's worse, we still can't figure out how in the world it got to this point.

We have started to silently live in our own private misery. A few glasses of wine may help us from thinking about the relationship, or perhaps this would be a good time to exact revenge and have an affair. Why are we so unlovable, we wonder? We may no longer have our self-confidence, self-respect, pride or dignity, but we sure as hell are going to hold onto the only thing we have left in this crazy mess: hope.

PULLING AWAY

The Love Addict may be going back and forth in her mind about whether or not *she* should pull away and cause the Commitment Phobe to feel the loss and gain some perspective to appreciate her again. However, she is afraid that this will cause him to run and just give up, never looking back. Nothing could be further from the truth. This guy doesn't want to lose her and will chase her if she pulls away. But this is not a safe game to play because it will just prolong the end of this relationship and drag it further into the depths of dishonesty.

EXCUSES, EXCUSES

After perpetuating the lie that life is less painful being in a relationship with a Commitment Phobe than being utterly and completely alone in this big scary world, we begin to make up excuses for his (and our) sneaky behavior. Everything becomes easier when we make excuses. For us Love Addicts, this can sometimes appear as a much more viable solution than dealing with pending pain and loss.

We (the Love Addicts) start to convince ourselves that the Commitment Phobe works a lot and we should not be so needy. After all, who are we to take away his financial stability and exceptional work ethic? That is, if lover boy really is at work.

And what about stress? Didn't he already have plenty of it?

We wouldn't want to rock the proverbial relationship boat when he already has so much to contend with in his life. After all, he would surely do the same for us. Right?

Making a list, written or mental, is a favorite Love Addict pastime.. We begin taking an inventory of the Commitment Phobe's actions. However, instead of making a proper list of all the negative effects he creates in this relationship to see our way out of this, we keep track of the once-in-a-blue-moon love note, gift, affection or sweet word that rolls off his otherwise sharp and lazy tongue. We survive on these little events as if they were the oxygen to our happiness. For every dozen horrific episodes, we read that one love note to keep our self-image afloat until the next fix.

HIS POTENTIAL

Ah, *potential*. What a dangerous little word we

use to keep us hoping. He looks good on paper, our parents love him and he is really sweet when things are "good." We just connect on so many levels, and he has so much potential to be a great partner! We forget that his issue is not the fact that he has OCD, leaves wet towels on the floor or smokes the occasional cigarette. No. His issue is *the relationship*. If only he were capable of loving us, then this relationship would be perfect! This is when some of us open our eyes before doomsday sets in, while others continue to look at his *potential* in hopes that he will one day magically wake up and acquire all of the basics that he lacks: loyalty, honesty, communication and respect.

MACKENZIE'S STORY

Length of Relationship: *Two years and two months.*

Commitment Phobic Attributes: *Shutdown, pornography addicted, irresponsible.*

"Hope can be a dangerous thing when attempting to change the behavior of a Commitment Phobe," I remember telling Mackenzie on her third visit to my office. She had just explained that she sent her magic angels over to him to help him see the light and notice how good the relationship was. If only he would let her love him and stop beating around the bush. Mackenzie was one of many clients who waited for her ex-boyfriend, Vincent, to miss her and come back.

"Looking at this scenario objectively," I asked, "does this seem fair to you?"

Mackenzie's lack of self-esteem was taking a toll on her as the days passed without Vincent. After several weeks, Mackenzie agreed it was time to move on and grieve the loss of her once knight in shining armor. She turned her focus back onto herself and started creating a new woman full of self- respect and independent love. After a few short months of self-reflection and inner work, Mackenzie was having a blast and celebrating a friend's birthday at a local restaurant when her phone rang. She looked down, saw Vincent's name on the screen and hit the "Decline" button on her phone with an feeling of nothingness. She felt vindicated, and two years later, she married a man who gave her his heart.

Ironically, his name was also Vincent. Fate did have a sense of humor after all.

CHAPTER 8

Extracurricular Activities

"Feed your own ego. I'm busy."

- Unknown

When the Commitment Phobe starts to panic about becoming too close to the Love Addict, he begins to delegate his time to other matters. At the same time, the Love Addict starts feeling ignored, rejected, abandoned or angry.

Warning signs that the Commitment Phobe is pulling away can vary from the minuscule to the extreme. Because the Commitment Phobe avoids intimacy at all costs, the very thought of it can send him straight into the mental institution. The following escapisms are all variables to which this guy may be susceptible. The Commitment Phobe can distract himself with work, friends, pornography, drugs and alcohol, gaming or computer addictions, to name a few.

THE EGO

The Commitment Phobe tends to pay much more attention to the desires of his ego than to his *real* inner self. He fuels his need for attention with women, giving him a much-needed boost to his self-esteem. Drawing attention in his direction can help quench his thirst and scratch that itch. It may not matter who or how; this guy takes it however he can get it, often manipulating the Love Addict into believing he's a perfect angel. The Commitment Phobe doesn't have the slightest idea on how to offer that love to himself, therefore, seeking it from others is his only hope for sustaining his continually waning sense of self.

WORK

Diving into work or becoming a workaholic can be a telltale sign of the Commitment Phobe's need to escape. In this case, the workaholic would prefer to spend the majority of his time away from the home, where commitment and pressure can threaten to spark his dormant fears.

The Commitment Phobe feels pressure to be the man that the Love Addict wants him to be, but he can't quite meet her expectations. He will sometimes stay at work until the wee hours of the morning or until she is fast asleep, leaving her unable to ask any questions or engage in intimate conversation. He especially does not want her to ask him for sex, a true mark of the beginning of the end.

PORNOGRAPHY

Often, the Commitment Phobe secretly loves pornography and can't get enough of it. This is sometimes shocking to you, the Love Addict, who may find out that this is why your guy usually isn't having much sex within the relationship. After a while, it becomes a fight to the finish just to get this man to go to bed with you.

Let's be honest. A little pornography never killed the cat.

Unless, of course, that cat is the Love Addict, and the pornography is in excess of hours upon hours a week at the hands of the Commitment Phobe. This guy gets an enormous sense of temporary relief from his duties as husband/boyfriend/lover by watching his favorite films starring *RainBlow Bright* and *Holly GoTightly*. The Commitment Phobe knows he does not have to be intimate with these fictitious women, making it easier for him to commit to the job at hand (no pun intended). This added release only aids in his already waning sexual desire for you.

SUBSTANCES

I am certainly not qualified to be an addiction specialist, but I do know that secrets can trigger addictions . When a person does not fully come to realize their past healthily, they will find whatever means possible to keep from being found out. Whether that secret is abuse, neglect, abandonment, trauma or commitment phobia, the need to disconnect from his own emotions, problems and past can sometimes lead the Commitment Phobe down a dangerous path. Not all addicts are commitment phobic, and I certainly don't want to generalize about addiction. However, this guy, much like an addict, feels the need to push down his feelings and disconnect from the reality that is screaming at him to confront. Alcohol abuse or excessive drinking can sometimes be prevalent in the Commitment Phobe for these reasons.

GAMING

This is one of my favorites because there is not a red flag that shines brighter and higher than a grown man playing some stupid video game for hours on end. Whether it is sports, fantasy worlds, building towns or shooting up his enemies, many Commitment Phobes choose this child-like outlet as an escape from their crumbling reality.

Gaming, of any kind, is likened to an addiction and can offer an escape from everyday reality, feelings and overwhelming emotions. Gambling would also be in this category. It's important to note that addiction can have many forms, and the online gaming industry is making a killing from grown men who suffer from commitment phobia. This is an easy (and safe) outlet for suppressing their pasts or fears.

THE SAMPLER PLATTER

Some of us are just lucky enough to enjoy all of the possible traits of the Commitment Phobe. When he cheats, he lies; when he wants to pull away, he games. When he is no longer interested in making love to us, he uses porn. All of these escapisms can prevail in one Commitment Phobe, and sometimes all extracurricular activities make an appearance within the same relationship.

This is what I like to refer to as the Extreme Commitment Phobe, and the Love Addict who is lucky enough to capture this man's attention is in for the ride of her life. This rocky relationship can go on and off for years, causing the Love Addict to become severely depressed yet unable to live without this guy. These two become a miserable duo, constantly blaming the other for their unhappiness, and neither one taking personal responsibility for their own issues.

MARYANNE'S STORY

Length of Relationship: *One year and ten months.*

Commitment Phobic Attributes: *Gaming, avoiding, disappearing.*

Remember that video game, World of Warcraft? Well, Maryanne does. She could tell you how to build wizard-like characters, slay dragons, steal gold (for real dollars!), plant flags and even get to level 70 before the week's end. Her boyfriend, Brad, taught her the ropes after she grew irritated with his cool, new avoidance technique. If you can't beat him, join him, she rationalized. Of course, it wasn't at all like this at first. Brad was once a loving partner with depth, and he contained that secret ingredient she had been looking for in all the others: connection.

But things had changed, and so had Maryanne. She would wake up in the middle of the night and find Brad at the computer, stabbing elves, shooting lions and mixing magic potions. She wasn't sleeping much those days because she just couldn't put her finger on what was going on with her once perfectly happy other half.

After months of gaming, Brad and the dragons left the relationship virtually overnight, leaving Maryanne confused and alone. She couldn't eat, couldn't sleep and couldn't figure out why Brad didn't embrace the connection that they clearly once had. When she finally moved on and learned that she had created Brad in her life for a reason, Maryanne started to see the light and realized her feelings of abandonment would always be triggered if she didn't deal with them head-on. And so she did. The following year, she met a man who loved her as much as she knew

CHAPTER 9

The Commitment Phobe's Double Life

"Always trust your gut feelings, as they never lie the way people do."

- Unknown

Jekyll and Hyde may technically be fictitious characters from long ago, but they can become prominent fixtures in the life of a Love Addict. The unpredictable aspects of the Commitment Phobe's daily life can make it hard to know what is driving his strange behaviors. Suddenly, this guy appears to have hidden agendas that don't seem to include his main squeeze. What is happening inside his complicated mind can cause the most intelligent woman to question her sanity.

There is a wide range of emotional justifications driving the Commitment Phobe to stray from his once cozy relationship. But one thing we know for sure is that being a mind reader has become our second job.

FLIRTING

Okay, I know what you are thinking: *all men flirt.* While this may certainly be true in small, innocent doses, the Commitment Phobe will use that justification as his Get Out of Jail Free card.

Many healthy couples (two individuals who love and respect each other) are comfortable with harmless flirtation outside of the relationship because trust and honesty lie at the foundation.

In her gut, the Love Addict knows when a line has been crossed, but trusting her own nagging intuition has become like an emotional game of hide-and-seek. As the relationship continues, she will naturally begin to question any instinct she ever had. The Love Addict will usually end up undermining her own value, subconsciously excusing his erroneous behavior around other women. But the Commitment Phobe doesn't usually innocently flirt, he is typically looking for something more.

Flirting can be a healthy way of expressing our basic feelings of sexuality, but when it goes on relentlessly behind our backs and without our approval, it can feel deceptive and hurtful. When

95

our self-worth is intact, we know the difference between innocent flirtations and blatant disregard for our

feelings and wishes.

Many times, the Love Addict may encounter online infidelity from various social networking websites . Some attempts at covering up these online infidelities may include:

I don't know her. I think maybe we went to high school together.

Nothing is going on. She has a boyfriend.

She is the one who keeps contacting me.

You want me just to ignore her? I don't want to hurt her feelings.

CHEATING

Let's be honest here. I could dedicate an entire chapter to cheating, and frankly, I had planned on it. And if Ross Geller were here, he would proclaim, "we were on a break" when confronted with rumors of deception. However, I find that cheating, as devastating as it is to the relationship, is still just a symptom of commitment phobia. It is important to note here that as much as his cheating makes you feel insecure, ugly and unwanted, it actually has nothing to do with you or with his feelings for you. It is solely related to his need for thrill and excitement away from the relationship and his fears of being enmeshed. Being with another woman gives him relief. In fact, a good indicator of a cheating Commitment Phobe is when things suddenly and out of nowhere are great within the relationship, and meanwhile, nothing you were aware of had even happened to change things. This is because after infidelity, the Commitment Phobe feels safer to open up to his love-addicted mate and become more intimate.

Where there's smoke, there's fire, and if the Commitment Phobe cheated once, he will do it again. We have all heard about the guy who accidentally tripped and fell into some woman's vagina or woke up at a party with a girl sucking on his private parts. *The horror*, he told you! *Can you believe the gall of such a slut?* (And of course, you can't, but you do.) I mean, our guy is desirable, so who could blame them, right? This is *our* guy we are talking about here. The one we wouldn't give the time of day to back in the pre-beginning because he could use a haircut, new clothes and a nose job. But, yes! It would make perfect sense that he spent the evening fending off some strange girl at a party with a bat. Believable. Totally.

We know now that studies show men think about sex every seven seconds. If this is the case, then the Commitment Phobe thinks about it every four seconds , and most women think about it every other Tuesday. But what drives the Commitment Phobe to extremes? When the Commitment Phobe feels the natural pull to be autonomous, he sometimes mistakes that urge for wanting to have sex with other women or a sign that you must not be The One. Go figure! He suddenly feels a need to get away, and he doesn't understand why. In fact, he often blames the Love Addict for pushing him.

Often a Love Addict will stay with a cheater because they "have a past" together. If your favorite coffee manufacturer stops making your favorite coffee, you are not going to call the company and say, "But we had a past!" The Love Addict feels that if she doesn't stay with the Commitment Phobe then she will have somehow wasted her time. Hence, she sticks around, attempting to make it work because she doesn't want to start all over again. Another reason the Love Addict stays is out of fear that she will be alone, as if that would be worse.

When it comes to cheating, this already tumultuous love affair can often turn into a veritable nightmare for the Love Addict. If there were only some way to keep him wanting, begging and pleading for her affections, she would surely try it, right? The Love Addict sometimes thinks that lingerie, soft porn, candlelight dinners or surprise morning romps will keep the Commitment Phobe from straying.

While I don't condone cheating, I am a strong supporter of forgiveness. Forgiveness frees us of resentment that will eventually build and kill any semblance of a relationship within ourselves. Forgiveness is for us, not them. Whether we stay in or leave the relationship, we can choose to be free from old resentments that cause unwanted anger or bitterness.

Compassion leads to forgiveness because we can see the perpetrator as a victim himself. We should, therefore, find compassion for a guy who can't let love in or out. Forgiveness is good. The issue of forgetting is a whole other story.

LIAR, LIAR

For the Commitment Phobe, the only intentional act second to lying is brushing his teeth. With all of the lies you find coming from his minty clean mouth, it's hard to tell if he really did have French toast for breakfast or scrambled eggs. Believing anything this guy says is starting to become a challenge. If you are one of the many women who is in search of truth and justice, this is usually when you become the FBI's next Scully-in-the-making. You are suddenly skilled at deciphering e-mails, texts, phone calls, phone bills, drive-bys and Newton's Law.

Because the Commitment Phobe is typically self-centered, self-righteous and self-absorbed, he is also the world's greatest liar. So much so that he often believes his own lies. This guy will lie about almost anything. Strangely, the Commitment Phobe leads a double and sometimes even a triple life. He doesn't know that lying is deceitful and can cause harm to others. He only knows that lying will get him out of any sticky situation, and because this guy may have spent years with other Love Addicts who put up with this type of behavior, he is taught that it works like a charm.

Eventually, the Commitment Phobe starts to thrive on his own lies, and the lying itself becomes its own monster. Sooner or later, you simply begin to question everything that comes out of this man's mouth.

PRIORITIES

Where once you could not care less about your man going over to Junior's house for a drink, you now shudder at the mere sound of guys night. You may or may not have a clue at this point why you cannot trust him. It may be due to actual infidelity or your fancy detective work of accumulated lies (like that naked photo or his ex's number on his cell phone).

After putting up a bit of a fight, you reluctantly let him have his space with the guys and continue to spend your night in panic, suspicion and upset that he is not where he says he is. If you call him to check his actual whereabouts, he may call you crazy and accuse you of being too jealous and controlling. So, scratch that. Instead, you decide to fume, guesstimate and play games with your mind. Ah, the mind. What a tangled web it weaves. In retrospect, this free time you had would have been better spent attempting an exorcism on the neighbor's cat.

Not long after his behavior gets even stranger, you realize the relationship is in dire straits, and you will do whatever you have to do to save it, including letting him have a guy's night out every time he's supposed to have plans with you. But no matter how drastic the attempt to "make nice," the Commitment Phobe somehow finds a way to ruin it.

Eventually, the Love Addict becomes a distant seventh to the Commitment Phobe's work, friends, family, home, pet and favorite television show. When it comes down to it, this guy cares mostly about himself and his own security and well-being, usually at the expense of anyone around him. When we are not busy pulling the wool over our own eyes, we can clearly see that we are just chilling out on the back burner of the Commitment Phobe's suddenly packed calendar.

A SNEAKING SUSPICION

By this point, we have either taken our heads out of the sand or chosen to leave them there. Whatever the decision, something is nagging at us that all is not what it appears to be in Lovers Cove . We may smell a rat, but if the rat isn't biting us then what is the harm? Clearly, confronting the Commitment Phobe only causes damage to the relationship, and God knows this thing only has so many lives. Leave it alone, we justify as we make our pros and cons list. Leave it alone, we insist to ourselves as 3 o'clock in the morning rolls around and still no phone call. Leave it alone; we will just make it worse, we concur. Leave it alone until we see actual proof. Why are we being so paranoid? We should really learn to trust more. This is all our fault.

It's self-talk like this that causes our nerves to fray and catapults us into a downward spiral, leading us to think we are the crazy ones. If we let our fears get the best of us, we will eventually tolerate more and more from the Commitment Phobe until not only did we once excuse his open flirtation with his sexy co-worker, but now we think his current shutting down and walling off is not as bad as that co-worker drama!

Boy, we sure lucked out. At least we're still together, we think...

LAURA'S STORY

Length of Relationship: *Ten Months.*

Commitment Phobic Attributes: *Lying, flirting, denying.*

In the midst of a divorce from a Commitment Phobe who had intermittent affairs throughout the relationship, Laura decided to lean on her rebound, John, for extra comfort and eventually began a relationship. John was a firefighter with the body to match, and although he had never had a relationship lasting more than two years, Laura was smitten and almost immediately forgot about her ex-husband.

John's favorite pastime was trashing his ex and rolling his eyes at his mother's phone calls. About six months into the relationship, Laura was at the computer and noticed John had left his Facebook account open. After having had a gut feeling for the past few weeks, not surprisingly, Laura opened his page with very little hesitation. As she perused his messages, it didn't take her long to find a handful of cyber-flirtations with a few unknown women. Some had replied, and some had ignored his advances.

While John was clearly feeling restless in his current relationship with Laura, he was just as confused as she was when she confronted his online indiscretions head-on. He was unhappy and didn't know why, and she was fuming and knew just the reason. But how was John going to get out of this relationship that he was feeling so suffocated in? Surely, he wasn't going to communicate with her about his fears and what he was going through. He had an even better idea!

After nine months, John left Laura with no explanation. He ended up shacking up with his ex-girlfriend, another Love Addict. This was his answer to feeling restless. Laura realized that if she had trusted her instincts from the start, she could have given herself time to grieve the loss of her relationship and heal.

CHAPTER 10

Manifestations of Commitment Phobia

"I'm pretty committed to our non-committal relationship."

- Unknown

The bad may outweigh the good at this point in the relationship, and you find yourself literally living for the good moments, which are now few and far between. But when they do happen, you hold onto them like a broken record , replaying the memories over and over until the Commitment Phobe disappears again, either emotionally or physically. You are now becoming that problematic couple, and you would do anything to find your Prince Charming, who you believe is buried underneath all of this drama.

While living his double life, the Commitment Phobe may have trouble hiding the consequences of his actions, however noble his attempts. Eventually, the Love Addict begins to see the signs that her Prince Charming may be up to no good. His strange behavior manifests as episodes that are difficult to be around. These episodes have a wide range and can vary from love and affection to avoidance and cruelty.

Arguing, shutting down, blaming others, acting irresponsibly or counting on his backup gal are just a few examples of how the Commitment Phobe's fears can manifest into episodes. At this point, you are officially asking yourself how in the Sam Hill this relationship got so far off track. It's time to buckle your seat belt because the best is yet to come.

SABOTAGE

The Commitment Phobe's feelings of enmeshment cause him to simultaneously sabotage the relationship, putting even his own happiness in harm's way.

Where the Love Addict feels the relationship is thriving, the Commitment Phobe feels stress and pressure as his own fears begin to surface. Often when the Commitment Phobe is happy and the relationship is running smoothly, he questions his feelings and whether or not they are valid, sabotaging the good that is around him.

Is she The One?

Why is she trying to suffocate me?

How am I going to handle another set of feelings when I can't handle my own?

What does she see in me? How can I get out of this?

What if I leave her and change my mind?

Why don't I feel the same way as I did in the beginning?

While the Commitment Phobe busies himself by appearing confident and cool, he is more often drowning inside and having sleepless nights over his deep feelings of inadequacy, unworthiness and self-loathing. He may feel disgusted with himself and can't figure out why. Because many of these guys spend much of their adult lives lying, deceiving, tricking and cheating, they clearly lack integrity, hence blocking their own road to happiness. Deep feelings of insecurity and inadequacy can keep the Commitment Phobe from wearing his heart on his sleeve and returning the love.

When he feels close to the Love Addict, he will sabotage any intimacy that was just created. The closer he gets to her, the more he will pull away. It is somewhat of a self-fulfilling prophecy: as the Commitment Phobe thinks the relationship is doomed, it *becomes* doomed. Instead of working to fix the relationship, he simply believes it should fix itself.

Due to his lack of communication skills, he does not express his fears to the Love Addict. Instead, he simply finds a way to sabotage any previous connection until he feels the need to be close once again.

THE INTENTIONAL FIGHTER

Everything was going so well, you told yourself. And now, every time you spend a wonderful evening together, feel his warm affection once again and finally have a breakthrough, the Commitment Phobe generates a massive commotion by creating such a debilitating fight, the half-dozen psychics on your speed dial couldn't have even predicted it.

Uncomfortable when things are headed in a healthy direction (toward a bigger commitment), this guy puts up his dukes in a way that even Mike Tyson wouldn't see coming, and when the Commitment Phobe wants to have a fight with the Love Addict, there is absolutely nothing she can do to stop it from happening. She may even recall agreeing with him completely, and he would still find a way to create friction and explode the conversation into full-blown World War Three. This can be very aggravating to the Love Addict, who thinks her soul mate has fallen off the deep end.

If the Commitment Phobe is the fighting kind, he has a good reason. Once he perpetuates an argument with the Love Addict, he has an instantaneous reason to justify pulling away and crawling back into his cave, spending time with other women or basking in his independence.

SHUTTING DOWN

Yes, *no*, *I don't know* and *whatever* become the Commitment Phobe's favorite words. When the going gets good, the Commitment Phobe shuts down. If all else fails, he will simply avoid you. This is due to several reasons. He may be feeling guilty about his childish behavior or latest infidelity, or he could be looking for a way to gain space after a recent intimate connection with you. He also may be thinking about leaving the relationship but can't commit to that either.

Any way you look at it, the Commitment Phobe

will do whatever it takes to avoid confrontation, communication and intimate connection. He works harder than Richard Nixon to bury his and the relationship's issues. Shutting down for the Commitment Phobe may mean he is simply not speaking, giving one-word answers, disappearing for a few days or weeks, blaming you or throwing a tantrum. Whatever manifestations of his emotional immaturity, they are guaranteed to cause more harm than good. And each time this guy pulls away, he is gone for a longer period of time.

THE BACKUP

Ironically, the Commitment Phobe does not like to be alone. He fears growing old without a good partner and is uncomfortable when left to his own devices. For this reason, he has to have a safety net to set his mind at ease. This can come in the form of an ex-girlfriend, a new lover or even just an online flirtation that he believes could later grow into a relationship given proper time and attention.

When the Commitment Phobe is without a woman as a backup (whether imagined or real), he is uncomfortable and feels even *less* committed to you than he normally does, triggering his irrational fears of enmeshment and loss of oxygen. In essence, what is really being triggered are his fears of abandonment, intimacy or making the wrong choice.

When he does have someone on the side, or if he has recently cheated, the Commitment Phobe becomes kind and loving again, almost out of nowhere! Remember the old anecdote of getting flowers from a man, and your response is, "*Now* what did you do?" Quite a ways into the relationship, you begin to smell a rat when he is suddenly showering you with kisses, making promises of the future (this is usually when he pops that awesome promise ring on your finger) and even having sex with you for the first time in ages.

The Commitment Phobe can be more intimate and available because subconsciously (I know that's getting old) he feels free from the possibility of being abandoned. In a sense, there is someone else's bed that is giving him relief from his main relationship with you. I like to call this *balancing*.

This makes no sense to the Love Addict because she believes the opposite should be true: a normal, healthy man would be tortured and riddled with guilt if he were seeing another woman behind her back. She would think he would be happiest when he was *not* cheating. But the Commitment phobe is not a normal, healthy committable man. He fears being alone, is not in touch with his feelings and avoids confronting his past.

THE BLAME GAME

The only thing the Commitment Phobe knows is that he is miserable and temporarily wants out of the relationship, blaming you in the process either verbally or silently. But the Commitment Phobe often does not see that he has too many faults because he would find it far too painful to look deep within himself. He fears doing so could open up a can of emotional worms, and it is far easier just to point the finger and move on. If the Commitment Phobe plays the blame game, you probably know just what it's like to defend yourself from a sudden and unexpected attack.

Don't think for a moment that this guy enjoys taking responsibility for his part in *anything*. You are the one who caused the fight, is needy, is difficult and PMSing, and you are certainly the one who is crazy. (At this point, we can't really argue with that one.) And whatever you did to piss him off last spring, he remembers it and will place that blame directly on you.

For the Commitment Phobe, it is important that you, the Love Addict, equally feel the heat. He is certain to point out your imperfections to take the spotlight off of himself and deflect responsibility for his behavior. Just when you least expect it, you suddenly become the "cheater" because back in 1985 (decades before you met), you sent a flirtatious letter to some ex-lover who is now your buddy, or you kissed some idiot one night after you learned of a severe cheating marathon at the hands of the Commitment Phobe. Your once tiny indiscretion is now being compared to his serious infidelities, and every time you bring up his continuing behaviors, he deflects the problem right back onto you, playing the part of the victim. This guy just loves deflecting the issues to avoid being labeled the "bad guy." And what's worse, you have fallen for his trick and suddenly find yourself defending your 1985 love letter as if your life depended on it! His deflection has worked, and he knows his manipulation has gotten the best of you.

The scariest part of the Commitment Phobe's

manipulations is that you may begin to believe that he is right. You begin to re-think everything: your words, your actions, your indiscretions, your lies, your accountability, your past, your future and your general internal concept of yourself. This can be the most dangerous of times because this is when you lose yourself and morph into the defensive victim. But alas, you concede.

IRRESPONSIBILITY

The Commitment Phobe has a hard time dealing with his own feelings and, therefore, cannot easily take responsibility for his actions and behaviors. He rarely apologizes unless provoked or backed into a corner. Many Commitment Phobes are simply unable to take responsibility for what happens in their own lives. He could be the CEO of a company or work in the mailroom. The Commitment Phobe's job status has nothing to do with his inability to take personal responsibility for his actions.

Sometimes it can appear as if anything that happens to this guy is someone else's fault. He just can't commit to taking responsibility. If the cable gets shut off, he blames the company and not his late payment. When he gets into an accident, it's not because he was wasn't paying attention to the road; it was the other guy's fault. When he loses his job, his boss is ironically the asshole. And when his relationship with the Love Addict ends, it is usually her fault for being too needy, too mean and too crazy. The Commitment Phobe may pull out the "it's not you, it's me" card, but internally he blames you for no longer being his picture of perfection.

The main reason for this failure to admit being wrong is due to the Commitment Phobe's fear of feeling bad, guilty or, generally, anything at all. He does not know how to allow it in because his boundaries are severely damaged. His inability to allow himself to feel much of anything (including your love) keeps him from taking responsibility. However, the consequences are always there, waiting for him when he finally decides to open his eyes.

In the *beginning*, you don't notice this silliness. The Commitment Phobe's secrets and lies are kept hidden from the Love Addict. In retrospect, you can see that there were small signs of his irresponsibility and victim stance, but the way he explained his side of the story always made sense to you. And on top of that, you would never shy away from the opportunity to be his shoulder to cry on when someone else has wronged him. You live for that! I mean, who are you to judge, right? After all, you're human. At least, this is what you told yourself.

Responsible men didn't really exist. And without his issues, you would not be able to be such a great caretaker!

EXTREME BEHAVIOR

When the Commitment Phobe has much deeper issues or has been lying, deceiving and lacking in integrity for a long time, more extreme behaviors can manifest. This type of Commitment Phobe has no empathy and cannot recognize others' emotions. This lack of compassion for those around him can be dangerous, both mentally and physically. These types of men are much more self-destructive.

A more extreme Commitment Phobe thrives on drama, making it nearly impossible for him to simply relax. His incessant need to worry and complain, either silently or verbally, creates emotional stress that wears down his sense of self and integrity. Emotionally immature and in denial of his reality, this guy often feels like the ground could fall out from under him at any given moment. His confusing and mysterious ways can make you feel like Scooby-Doo trying to figure out who is under the ghost.

LIZ'S STORY

Length of Relationship: *Eleven Months.*

Commitment Phobic Attributes: *Fighting, blaming, deflecting.*

Liz and her boyfriend Troy were in bed one night, cuddling and watching reruns of their favorite show, *Breaking Bad*. He whispered, "I love you" in her ear as he fell into a deep sleep.

Liz was on cloud nine as this was the first time she had heard this statement from his mouth. She fell asleep on Troy's chest, dreaming of their bright future.

The next morning, Liz was in her kitchen doing the dishes when Troy came in and sat down at the kitchen table. He was silent at first, and then he opened his mouth.

"Why do you use so much soap when you wash the dishes? It's a waste," Troy said, clearly irritated.

Liz didn't exactly get the greeting she had hoped for. After all, she was too distracted naming their children. But Liz knew this abrupt attitude was a possibility as Troy had the tendency to pull back after getting too close in the past.

"Oh, I see. You're pretending you can't hear me. Figures," he added.

Liz didn't understand the rules of arguing with a Commitment Phobe: silence. But for whatever reason, that last word was sticking to her like glue.

"Figures *what*?" she demanded.

"You aren't interested in this relationship," quipped Troy. "You enjoy ignoring me just like you did at Terry's party last year when you were chatting it up with her brother."

Here we go, thought Liz. The infamous "Terry's brother" argument. *Why couldn't he just get over this*, she thought. After all, she had already apologized a million times.

"Are you serious? Why are you bringing this up now, after the amazing night we had last night?" She asked. "I thought we settled this already. I'm sorry, babe. I didn't mean to hurt you. I was just talking to him. That was all."

Liz was desperately trying to stop this train from running her over, but the conductor was having none of it.

"Talking? He was almost petting your breasts with his eyes! I saw the way he looked at you. You're such a liar." Troy stood and began to collect his belongings. "You should really think about why you are with me when you obviously think about other men."

And with that, he scurried from the kitchen to the bedroom and eventually to the hallway. As he opened the front door, Troy gave Liz one last disapproving look before slamming it on his way out.

Furious at his outrageous behavior, Liz was also riddled with disappointment. Her perfect night had been ruined, and she only had herself to blame. After all, she was flirting with Terry's brother last year, and he was still hurt over her indiscretion, right?

Wrong.

Troy's pre-planned argument was a path to an

escape route. When he awoke that morning, he felt enmeshed and suffocated by the events of the prior evening. He wanted to breathe and didn't even really know why. But instead of explaining this to Liz, he acted out like a child and made sure she knew it was her fault.

Troy was not upset about Terry's brother; he just knew that making her look like the perpetrator was the only way he could play the victim. Well aware that Liz had done no wrong, Troy was hellbent on turning the tables and buying a little space from this relationship at the cost of Liz's feelings. Because Liz was a Love Addict, she was immediately worried about Troy's dramatic upset.

Almost a week went by before Troy called, and without apologizing, he asked Liz out to dinner where they relit the old spark. If Liz's self-worth were at a healthy level, she would have told Steve to shove his dinner up his you-know-what. But she was so happy he finally called that all logic or reason flew out the window. Liz was overjoyed by what she thought was her renewed love for Troy. Until the next time he brought up Terry's brother.

CHAPTER 11

Manipulating for Love

"If our emotional stability is based on what other people do or do not do, then we have no stability."
- Marianne Williamson, *Enchanted Love: The Mystical Power of Intimate Relationships*

At the manipulation stage of the relationship, we have almost lost who we were to this guy. Everything we do now seems to be in an effort to fix what has been broken and attempt to steer it back toward the *beginning*. This is around the time that many of us take up therapy or consider antidepressants.

As the Commitment Phobe slowly begins to pull away, the Love Addict searches for ways to lure him back in by acting aloof and uninterested. This forces the Commitment Phobe to think he is losing his leading lady or that she may have gotten over her needy ways.

At some point during this relationship, the Love Addict does what she knows best. She begins to manipulate the Commitment Phobe for attention afraid that he is losing his desire to be with her. These manipulations take many forms from making it seem as if there are other men to ignoring him until he comes around again. Some games may work in the short-term because, after all, the Commitment Phobe's innermost fear is loss and being alone. The Love Addict has only one mantra at this point: *Save the relationship.*

This impending feeling of doom, abandonment and rejection can be stronger than some chemical drug withdrawals, causing such emotional distress that it can sometimes lead us to wonder why there aren't more recovery centers for Love Addicts. The important piece to recognize here is that healthy relationships require no manipulation for love. Manipulating for love is like putting a Band-aid on a serious injury. The relief is only temporary and will only lead to more problems without intervention.

POWER STRUGGLE

At this stage, the Love Addict starts to crave any kind of "good feeling" she can get her little paws on. To feel even half as good as she once did, and while her self-esteem is taking a serious beating, she starts grasping for straws.. It's like a drug addict in need of a fix. Tired of feeling emotionally distraught and energetically depleted, she finds herself craving even the smallest amount of attention from the Commitment Phobe, even if that means she has to sink him down to sewer-level status to have him look up at her again.

Usually, in this push/pull relationship, one person is in power, and the other is shit out of luck. The Love Addict is the one who strives to have the power, and she will practice just about any manipulation to get it. On the other hand, the Commitment Phobe is usually unaware right up until the power is slipped out from underneath him, and he starts to crave more attention again.

A healthy relationship does not have an imbalance of power due to self-love and the mutual respect that the couple have for one another. They have no desire to see their partner as "below" them. When we find ourselves relieved because we are in charge of the playing field, we only set ourselves up for failure. Feeling like the ball is in our court, or feeling like we have the current "upper hand" is just a means to an end. This is our way of feeling good again and relieving pain in the moment, giving our ego a break from the previous time we just spent "on the bench" while the Commitment Phobe ruled the field (even though he wasn't actually trying). But it isn't long before we realize that this soccer game has only one player, and we will play to win, only losing more of ourselves in the process.

REPLACEMENT READY

The Love Addict tends to dot her i's and cross her t's when it comes to assuring that she will not be without love. Often moving from one guy to the next, she sees each new experience as an opportunity for love. When things are getting rather sticky with her partner, she secures a backup, and may even leave the Commitment Phobe for the new love interest. This infidelity just adds to the unhealthiness of the relationship and typically happens more than a year in, when the Commitment Phobe has been pulling away for quite some time.

Cheating is only a temporary relief from feeling like the underdog. Many times, when the Love Addict decides to look for acceptance outside of the relationship with the Commitment Phobe, she may even leave him for another one.

While cheating, the Love Addict may feel it is perfectly justified to feel desirable again and gain a leg up (no pun intended) on her self-esteem and waning ego. And once the Commitment Phobe catches on to the Love Addict's cheating ways, he will be sure to use it against her to make up for his own indiscretions. Our one night of hot sex will be his open-door excuse for all affairs past and future. Cheating is never the answer and will only diminish our self-worth, making the ego stronger and even more destructive.

By immediately starting a relationship with a new guy, this type of self-destruction keeps the Love Addict safe from looking at her own issues. She would rather attempt to get love from an outside source over and over again rather than give it to herself, continually taking the impossible way out.

THE VICTIM STANCE

The other manipulation game that runs rampant at this stage is self-manipulation. As we steadily crawl further into the depths of denial, we become masters at manipulating ourselves into believing this is just a "bad phase" in the relationship. These manipulations are the most dangerous because we start to believe maybe we're the ones with the problem. Perhaps we have been too needy, perhaps he is right, and we are "crazy" after all. We will do anything to avoid the pain of losing this guy (hard to believe after the way he clearly does not prioritize us), and we cannot bear the thought of being alone, single and flat-out wrong about our once steadfast prince.

When we take responsibility for what we do, think and feel, it automatically gives us the power to create a different future. We then take full responsibility for our happiness and well-being. The labels of "bad" and "good" that we have in our lives are only a function of what we are creating, however unintentional. It is important to take control of our creations and pay attention to what we are focusing on. The more we play games, the further we fall from grace.

In the victim stance, we lose the power to think, feel and do what is best for us. We have given all of the relationship power over to the Commitment Phobe and have ceased to be the decision-makers in our own relationship. *Why have I let him decide the fate of our relationship? Why is it all up to him? Where has my power gone?*

MUTUAL JUSTIFICATIONS

Both offending parties are guilty of justifying the other's unhealthy relationship habits. At this point, the Commitment Phobe feels perfectly justified in pulling away. After all, the Love Addict became a nag and even stopped rubbing his feet on Sundays. This guy is a pro at tossing the blame around and justifying his every action. He feels entitled to his video games, online flirtations, secrets and lies. He has pushed the Love Addict away and, in doing so, has created his own reasons for shutting her out. After all, he can't blame himself. That would require effort and responsibility. It is much easier for the Commitment Phobe to justify this way of life than to deal with what is underneath the behaviors.

The Love Addict has her own justifications to contend with. She doesn't want to lose her once Prince Charming, so she makes sure that she excuses his lack of respect, emotional abuse and silent treatments, often at the cost of her own self-esteem. When the Commitment Phobe backs away from sex, the Love Addict justifies that it's due to his low libido . Since when is that normal? At this point, we have the wool so tightly pulled over our eyes that we start to look like sheep.

We, the Love Addicts, feel that staying in the relationship is justified because of what we had in the *beginning*, and we would rather live on a wing and a prayer that one day the Commitment Phobe will wake up and remember the good times. We justify because we love him.

THE LOVE ADDICT'S FEAR

Most Love Addicts could get physically ill at the thought of their commitment-phobic Casanova rolling in the sheets with another woman. This can be reason enough to keep the Commitment Phobe in line and interested in her. She will go to great lengths to make sure he does not stray from their bedroom, including staying in this push/pull relationship. At the time, the Love Addict is not too concerned that this urge has little to do with actual love. In fact, the tolerance level of the Love Addict is so high at this point that she has given new meaning to the word "doormat."

In conjunction with the fear of losing the Commitment Phobe to another woman, the Love Addict does not want to feel as though her time was wasted on someone who was not going to join her in her "happily ever after." She may simply continue this relationship so that she feels she has not wasted any precious time.

Surviving a failed relationship is one thing, but having to face her family and friends is another. The Love Addict would sometimes rather save face in the event of losing the guy whom they may have once warned her about. Whatever the season, the Love Addict can find a million reasons to keep this guy around if it means avoiding confronting her own past and deep-rooted insecurities.

JESSIE'S STORY

Length of Relationship: *One year and nine months.*

Commitment Phobic Attributes: *Withholding affection, disappearing.*

Jessie got dressed up in her Sunday best and texted her boyfriend, Charlie, to inform him that she was in his neighborhood on business and was wondering if she could swing by. In actuality, she was just standing on her balcony waiting for him to text back, make-up ready. When he didn't reply, she went into a panic, nearly breaking down my office doors with mind-numbing anxiety.

Jessie's case was fairly typical. The relationship started out with utter elation and deep connection until he slowly pulled away, without ever fully letting her go. By the time Jessie was into manipulation mode, she no longer cared about her integrity. She only needed to relieve her anxiety. And as a former drug user and addict, men had become her heroin.

Charlie did call a few days later and asked Jessie to come over. She was relieved, but her manipulation hadn't worked as she planned. Instead, she decided to tell Charlie that an ex-boyfriend had been calling her. Unaware that the Love Addict can manipulate quite well, Charlie went into a rage, insisting that she tell her ex to cease and desist immediately. He spent the remainder of that evening holding Jessie close to him and whispering sweet nothings. The following week was business as usual: Jessie feeling ignored and Charlie doing the ignoring.

CHAPTER 12

I'm Confused/ I Understand

"If he's giving you mixed signals, the signal is clear."
- Unknown

This part of the relationship is the most disturbing because it is when we start to accept these troubling antics as normal relationship protocol. We begin to feel sorry for the man who has stepped over, under and on us during this push/pull tumultuous love fest. We are convinced that sacrificing ourselves for the betterment of the relationship is our job because, of course, we would do anything to get back to the *beginning*.

If the Commitment Phobe has expressed confusion and frustration, waning in and out of the relationship either emotionally or physically, we may start to see his confusion as an undiagnosed disability. So, we tell ourselves that we should have compassion because this poor little lost puppy is scared and has issues with insecurity and self-doubt. What kind of cold and callous bitch would leave this guy to his own devices? Not us! But before we make the soothing decision to fight for the man we met in the *beginning*, we both offer two phrases of encouragement to put each other at ease and to continue this soap opera: **I'm confused**, and *I understand*.

I'M CONFUSED

After the perpetual deceit, pulling away, impending affairs, lies and general unrest, the Commitment Phobe, a modern-day Christopher Columbus, stumbles upon a great and unexplored discovery: he is confused. Whatever led him to feel confused? My five-year-old niece could come to that discovery faster.

Not so ironically, the Commitment Phobe is genuinely confused at this point. This may be the one sure-fire truth he has offered you in quite some time, and you appreciate his honesty, however hurtful. You hang onto this truth because it feels good, it makes sense and it means there is a light at the end of this dark tunnel.

At this point, he may even reveal a bit about his

self-loathing, critical inner voice and unresolved feelings. The Commitment Phobe senses he is damaged goods and may often feel like a failure. He may even drag his adolescence, parents or death of his childhood dog, Fifi, into his outpouring of distress. You are listening with all five ears and hang onto every word with hopes of a reversal. Could this be the breaking point that transports us back to the *beginning*? He may even break down in tears over fear, guilt, shame or a cocktail of all three. This can give the Love Addict an artificial feeling of closeness.

The Commitment Phobe's admission to being confused is hurtful, but at the same time, a much-needed breath of fresh air. After all, we now have something to work with. At least we finally know how he feels! If the Commitment Phobe sheds some tears at this point, this is like gold to the Love Addict.

Our poor guy is sad! What kind of women would we be if we abandoned him in his time of confusion? I mean, we too have struggled with the disease of confusion and wouldn't have wanted to be abandoned because of it! Our response, naturally, is one of concern, love, support and friendship. We are there for him through thick and thin, even if that means utter unhappiness. But we are an adult, and most of all, we completely, utterly and unapologetically *understand*.

I UNDERSTAND

The English language has many words, but none as important to the Love Addict's vocabulary as "I understand." After being lied to, rejected, pushed and pulled, you have seen it all, and the truth is that you really are beginning to understand! But this understanding comes at a price.

Even though you are just as confused as to why *he* is so confused, you are not going to let that little detail derail you from the best response on the planet! "I understand" is, of course, the only understandable response to this. I mean, who on Earth isn't understanding when it comes to confusion?

Welcome to the Girlfriend of the Year Awards. Come on, this is no time to be shy! Don't be so humble! Get up here and collect your award! You have officially chosen to "stand by your man" and take it up the you-know-what until he figures out what in the world he wants out of life, you and a relationship! This is no time for humility.

You deserve this award. You have worked really hard for it! Plus, this is the only way you will be able to climb into your DeLorean, strap on your seat belt and set the odometer back to the *beginning*! And by golly, this was going to work, you told yourself. You were going to be the most understanding girlfriend or wife (yes, the Commitment Phobe can marry) and bring your guy back from outer space. Your Prince Charming is lost, and you are going to help map his way back to the promised land.

So, take that award and be proud. But remember, giving up yourself for a man comes at a high price, especially when there is no time machine to take you back to the *beginning*. After all, the *beginning* is in the past. But there's no need for additional scientific logic at this point. I think you know where I'm going without all of that time-warp, black-hole nonsense.

It's important to note that these divisive and pertinent roles of the confused man and the understanding woman can weave in and out of the relationship, even after it ends, and he works his way back.

ACTIONS VS. WORDS

While the Commitment Phobe is busy being con-

fused, and the Love Addict is understanding her day away, it's time to really think about how many things the Commitment Phobe has said that have actually come into play. We all know that actions speak louder than words, but seldom do we apply this to the Commitment Phobe. His inability to act on his words isn't personal. His words may be endearing, promising and sometimes uplifting, but the Commitment Phobe's actions usually say it all.

Paying attention to the Commitment Phobe's actions instead of his words can save the Love Addict a lot of time and headache. Remember, this is the same guy who wanted to meet our family but keeps having to work late...on a Sunday...in Iceland...on Christmas.

MIXED SIGNALS

Sometimes there is just no way to know what is going on in this guy's mind. He may say one thing and do another, but the most confusing of all is that this guy pursued *you*, and you continually plead your case to others so that they, too, understand your confusion:

But getting married was his idea!

He was the one calling me all the time. I barely dialed

his number! I was the one saying we should slow down.

He kept telling me that he wanted me to meet his parents. I wasn't the one bringing up moving in together!

No matter the time, day or year, the Commitment Phobe has a tale for all seasons. He talks a big talk while the Love Addict plays it cool as a cucumber. She knows what is best for her game while this guy truly believes he wants to do all of these magical things. But in just a matter of weeks or months, the Commitment Phobe's fear takes over, and the Love Addict finds herself...by herself.

STANDING BY YOUR MAN

At this point, you have officially convinced yourself that this poor guy is going through something or could even be depressed. But you are his biggest cheerleader, and come hell or high water, you will stand by your man. You are convinced that after this life transition and intermittent interruption of your love fest that he will eventually go back to the way he was in the *beginning*, if you can just stick around and support him through this difficult time.

But trying to get back to the *beginning* is now becoming less of a possibility, no matter how much you refuse to lose hope. You tell yourself that you know he is broken, but you can live with that. After all, isn't that what a supportive girlfriend does? Stand by her man? This is a dangerous point in the push/pull relationship. When you become the one who can save him, you enter another chapter with this guy. You have given yourself permission to stay. This is your way of justifying how he treats you, and if anyone can bring this guy back to his real self, it's you. The problem is not only does he not want to be saved, he starts to resent you waiting around and wonders why you are so fixated on being there to catch him when he falls.

I am not suggesting that we abandon our partners at the first sign of trouble or when hard times arise. However, when his "hard times" cause him to use us as his emotional or physical punching bag, there is a big difference. Standing by your man while sacrificing your integrity, self-worth, joy and pride is a sign that you are in too deep, and it is time to look at the big picture. Changing someone is just about the most futile stance any sane person can take. If we could change people, don't you think we would have peace on Earth?

THE CATCH

After you have graciously accepted your Girl-friend of the Year Award, you begin to realize that your mapping skills to follow this path that will hopefully lead you back to the *beginning* are not exactly working in your favor. They may even be backfiring. So, you start to look for a new map, and while you are busy googling things like compulsive liar, disconnected father and effects of losing a pet, all hell breaks loose. You find yourself wishing you had never shown weakness or vulnerability in those times of understanding. This must be the reason he finds you so undesirable!

The Commitment Phobe's confusion is temporary, like an earache or genital crabs, because he suddenly becomes very coherent when he gives into another girl's advances or spurts out another lie within just a few short hours. But these lies fit into the same category as his confusion.

Quite opportunistic, the Commitment Phobe sees your understanding nature as loving and an "open door" for future mistakes that will again inevitably be forgiven by such an understanding woman. You are so understanding because you have built up a tolerance for this ridiculous behavior and have lost all objectivity. All in the name of who he was in the *beginning*.

But the confusion and understanding don't last long, and if he has not left the relationship a few times already, he starts to feel the itch more strongly than ever. Your understanding nature, in essence, becomes another cross for him to bare.

CAROL'S STORY

Length of Relationship: *Four years.*

Commitment Phobe Attributes: *Cheating, sabotaging, blaming, on and off.*

Carol was the most understanding woman I had ever met. She knew that Adam had commitment issues and was very educated about his fears and insecurities. She was aware that he had some pain associated with his past and that he could not decide whether or not he even wanted a relationship. Against all logic and reason, she was willing to be the sacrificial lamb for the betterment of their relationship. She knew Adam was confused, even when she married him. And boy, was she really understanding.

When he went out of town and didn't call her for a whole week, she understood. When he shut down and blamed her, she understood. When he slept with his boss, she understood. When he asked for a divorce and then changed his mind a few weeks later, she was Little Miss Understanding.

Carol's need to be loved and accepted trumped any desire to be treated with dignity and respect. She tolerated a lot in her years with Adam and didn't stop to take responsibility for her part in the dysfunction. She was the typical, willing doormat and played the victim role quite well.

"What if there is no one else out there for me?" retorted Carol when I asked her point-blank why she continued to stay with Adam.

"I'm afraid no one else will want me and I will end up alone. Besides, I am so used to him that I can't imagine myself with anyone else."

When I gently tried explaining that she had control over her own life, her future and her choices and that she would not end up like the old lady in a shoe, Carol declared, "But I love him!"

Leaving her fate in Adam's hands, Carol was an emotional mess when Adam eventually moved out. He told her it was because she had flirtatiously texted with her coworker before they were ever married. As he sabotaged the relationship bit by bit, Carol had stuck to Adam like glue. They were a match made in heaven, and when he left her, he did so with gusto, making no apologies.

No matter how much Carol understood about Adam's commitment phobia, it wasn't enough to bring the relationship back to the *beginning*. It wasn't even enough to make it work in its current state. It turned out that the more Carol understood, the more she unknowingly damaged her own self-worth. She was willing to give up her happiness for Adam, a luxury she felt she could do without.

CHAPTER 13

Exit Strategies

"Fine, break up with me. I'm sure there's plenty of women out there just waiting to be partially pleased."

- Unknown

By the time the Commitment Phobe has disappeared, the Love Addict may have already seen it coming. But this doesn't seem to keep her from being dumbfounded. His feelings of enmeshment have caused him to cut and run for the hills, and there is nothing the Love Addict did, other than wanting to give and receive love that caused this downward demise of a tumultuous relationship. The Commitment Phobe would prefer that it somehow be the Love Addict's idea to leave the relationship, but on the off chance that he can't get her out the door by behaving like a total chicken, then he will resort to doing the dirty work. Even when it comes to breaking up, this guy still doesn't want to put the work in!

When the going gets good, the Commitment

Phobe gets going. Sometimes his fears are triggered by the relationship going very well. Unfortunately for the Love Addict (and the waning relationship), the Commitment Phobe is usually not aware that he is functioning out of fear instead of love.

The Commitment Phobe will rarely exit a relationship without having another woman waiting in the wings. This usually takes a while for the Love Addict to see clearly, but the Commitment Phobe does not enjoy being alone. This woman-in-waiting may be real or imagined. She may be an innocent online flirtation that he sees as a possible companion, or she may be an ex-girlfriend or a fly-by-night lover. Whoever she is, she is just another Love Addict in need of affection.

It is not common for the Love Addict to leave the Commitment Phobe unless forced or manipulated. Having a deep-seated fear of abandonment, being unloved and being alone, she will usually stay with this guy unless it has gotten so unbearable that she realizes she is simply just as miserable with or without him. In that case, she finds another Commitment Phobe to latch on to. Often sensing impending doom and rejection, the

Love Addict will beat him to the punch and hand the Commitment Phobe his walking papers just to avoid a bruised ego. The Love Addict may be so emotionally exhausted that she can't take it anymore, having spent months or even years trying to make this relationship work.

Even though the Love Addict would rather fix than end the relationship, she may decide it is better to leave with her dignity still intact. However, the majority of Love Addicts stay until the Commitment Phobe abandons them or pushes them to the edge.

In any event, it is somehow still surreal and shocking when the Commitment Phobe finally decides to exit the relationship. He may force you to leave him or cry about his confusion. He could be immersed in guilt or simply disappear into thin air. He may shoot you a cowardly text or e-mail. Whatever his exit strategy, the Love Addict is usually in for a treat when the Commitment Phobe makes his dramatic exit.

THE ARGUER

The fighter's strategy is the least fun of all because when the Commitment Phobe wants some relief away from the relationship, sometimes there is nothing a Love Addict can do to stop him from causing an argument. A big fight can give the Commitment Phobe an immediate excuse to exit, even just temporarily. The worst part is that you are literally and desperately trying to stop the train wreck before it occurs, and his tunnel vision has him dead set on having a fight. No matter how much you become agreeable to maintain the peace, this guy will persist, finding a way to blame you in the process.

Some Love Addicts proclaim that they have never had a fight with the Commitment Phobe. Contrary to what some may think, this is actually not a great sign. Arguing or disagreeing (however heated) can be signs that the parties involved care about the relationship enough to speak out. When the Commitment Phobe is cut off from his own feelings, there is no need to fight it out. He does not have the willingness to even work on the relationship.

THE DEFLECTOR

As I mentioned earlier , the Commitment Phobe is great at playing the blame game and getting you to think *you* are the problem. Because the Commitment Phobe is usually partaking in some form of deceit or infidelity, he knows that if he accuses you, the Love Addict, of cheating, you will certainly stand up on your hind legs and declare to the relationship gods that this is indeed bullshit. The Commitment Phobe knows this will not only deflect his deceptions but also render you defenseless against his carefully planned offense. He will bring up some obscure e-mail you received from an ex or remind you of some guy you said "hi" to in a library last winter. He knows exactly what he is doing and how defensive you will get. However, he is very clear that you did nothing wrong. This is just a cowardly way to make sure he puts a dent in a relationship that is too close to becoming intimate. Until, of course, he changes his mind once again.

The Commitment Phobe may believe that the end of the relationship was your fault, and that you did something wrong to ruin his perfect perception of you. He thinks he was trapped because you suddenly weren't the woman he fell in love with. And in a way, you weren't. In part, you have become this lackluster, passive and partially empty human being because so much of your energy had been wasted on trying to figure this guy out. This time-consuming drama and energy drain can eventually feel "normal."

THE MUTE

This exit strategy is my personal favorite because this guy doesn't have the skill or know-how to pull off the others so effortlessly. He is much too lazy, so he just shuts his mouth and hopes for the best. He doesn't have a better plan for getting rid of you, and he is counting on you getting irritated enough that you excuse yourself from the relationship. Until, of course, he changes his mind.

When a Commitment Phobe suddenly becomes an A-list actor from an old silent movie, it can be very annoying for the Love Addict. Giving the silent treatment was over in kindergarten, and this idiot wants to bring it back. As if there weren't enough communication problems in this relationship already, the Commitment Phobe thinks this tactic is a fitting end.

THE NICE GUY

This guy is few and far between, but once in a while the Commitment Phobe does the right thing and calls it quits in an adult-appropriate fashion. Usually lacking the confidence to do it in person, he may at least pick up the phone or send a text and explain that this relationship isn't working in the way it should (due to his utter lack of trying). After all the damage he may have caused, he usually decides that this is a fine time to become a stand-up citizen and do the right thing. The Love Addict is heartbroken, but this guy can change his mind at the drop of a hat because he can't live with you, and he can't live without you.

The Nice Guy says things like, "You deserve better" (which you do) and "I'm not good at this relationship thing" (which he's not). This guy has a bit of a conscience when it comes to the Love Addict's feelings and thinks that honesty may be the best policy.

THE HARRY HOUDINI

This disappearing act has such devastating consequences that it's hard for the Love Addict to fully recover. In *Men Who Can't Love*, authors Steven Carter and Julia Sokol refer to this "disappearing act" as one of the most emotionally detrimental ways in which the Commitment Phobe exits the relationship.

With his lack of communication skills and un-resolved fears, this type of Commitment Phobe simply doesn't want to deal with the real world. To avoid confrontation or temptation, this guy will sneak out the back door when you're fast asleep or simply refuse to pick up that phone af-ter a whirlwind romance. Whether two years or one day into the relationship, Houdini can per-form his final curtain call at any moment.

THE REENTRY

Just when you're beginning to recover, here comes Prince Charming, swaggering back in to soak up all of your self-esteem again because the Commitment Phobe can't commit to staying, and he can't commit to leaving. Sometimes hearing through the grapevine that you may have found a new man is enough to make the Commitment Phobe jump headfirst into damage control. He didn't have the emotional maturity to foresee the potential dangers and consequences of his deci-sion to break up with you, including the fact that you may move on.

But you are very understanding, and being a good little Love Addict, you throw down the wel-come mat (after you warned him not to do this

again, of course). The Commitment Phobe realizes he made a mistake because he, too, remembers the *beginning*, and he may have noticed that
the woman or women he dated after his departure were also not perfect. You can't believe your
ears: Is he really professing his love for you? Is
your Prince Charming back? He sure is! You are
finally back to the *beginning*, and he promised he
would never be so stupid again. Lesson learned!
Our guy. He's back. And with a good talking to,
he's all fixed.

Due to his subconscious fear of abandonment,
the Commitment Phobe can often be hard to get
rid of, even popping up years after the breakup,
wanting to pick up where he left off. He hates being alone, and his debilitating back-and-forth antics are enough to make any person *crazy* (a label
the Love Addict hears often from this guy). The
more you leave him alone and play your avoidance games, the quicker he may come running
back, only to do it all over again. After all, he
doesn't actually want to lose you for good! While
the Commitment Phobe has pulled away, he is
always sure to keep a foot in the door by leaving
personal items behind to ensure a place in your
future when he decides he misses you and your

annoying cat. Decisions are not his forte, and he certainly does not want to look back with regret.

The second time around, the Honeymoon Phase is so brief that if you blink, you may miss it. Before you know it, the entire push/pull cycle repeats itself and this time at lightning-fast speed. The chase, the *beginning*, the fight or flight and the dramatic ending occur within a shorter time frame. This mini version of your relationship can happen several times, and each time it seems he has changed. And once again, he is confused, and you understand.

He had spent the majority of his relationship with the Love Addict avoiding intimacy, albeit he was ready to commit now! While he was usually afraid of judgment when he showed his true self, he was now ready to open up. The Commitment Phobe may often be moved to tears on bended knee, virtually begging the Love Addict to give him another chance. This is a good sign that this guy has no idea what he wants and lives in a cloud of confusion, coming and going with the wind.

LILLIAN'S STORY

Length of Relationship: *One year and seven months.*

Commitment Phobic Attributes: *Chasing, lying, shutting down.*

Lillian was dying to get married in her mid-twenties, primarily looking to fit in and feel worthy of a man's love and commitment. She met Cal at a work event, and they hit it off instantly. He showered her with attention, texted all the time and generally won her over within just a few short weeks. Lillian was in love, and she wanted the world to know. One night after several cocktails and some bar hopping, she convinced Cal to elope, explaining that it would be fun and adventurous. He complied. After all, he truly wanted to get married. He wanted to commit! Living up to the commitment was another story.

After their classy little wedding in Las Vegas's Chapel of Love, the duo returned home to business as usual. During the next year, their relationship slowly unraveled, and Cal became more and more distant.

Lillian went out to have lunch with a friend only to return to a half-empty apartment to find Cal and all of his belongings gone. In utter shock, Lillian's knees buckled as she fell to the ground. It looked as though she had been robbed. A few days went by before she had enough logic and objectivity to realize that his escape had been planned well before her innocent luncheon. She knew this because she eventually noticed an empty space on the kitchen counter where the stainless-steel toaster had once been. Her ex's best friend gave them the toaster as a wedding gift. Lillian knew right then this was a two-man job, as her ex had never even used the toaster. This devious plan was far more than her brain could calculate at the time. She was too busy wondering what hit her and how her love and devotion just wasn't enough for him.

Part Two:
Behind the Mask

Behind the Mind

CHAPTER 14

The Aftermath

"Ruin is a gift. Ruin is the road to transformation."
- Elizabeth Gilbert, *Eat Pray Love*

After all is said and done, how the Commitment Phobe exited the relationship may not even matter. It's the confusion that you are left with. That delightful feeling of what the hell went wrong and what the hell just happened is what keeps you up at night. You're miffed. You can't breathe. Everything you thought you knew was wrong.

At the other end of this dark tunnel is the life that you were meant to live because, believe it or not, everything is perfect exactly the way it is. If this were not supposed to happen, it would not have happened. It is important to know that the universe is always looking for the best possible result in any given situation. Apparently, your best result was not having some jerk in your life. Be excited for what or who could come next, even if you only see a tiny light shining through the cracks. Amongst your pain, never let go of hope.

SHOCK AND AWE

The aftereffects of this relationship with a Commitment Phobe can be devastating and extremely disturbing, forcing us to question our innate instincts and judge of character. We spend the next several weeks in shock, wondering how such a perfect match in the *beginning* could suddenly get so off track. We started hoping he would see how good things could have been if he had simply opened his eyes and stopped sabotaging everything.

At this point, the Love Addict may even be comparing the ending of this relationship with the relationships of her past, looking for similarities. Could this really have happened *again*? We would have bet our unborn child that this guy was not like the others.

THE COMMITMENT PHOBE'S REGRET

After having *never* thought through his decision, the Commitment Phobe may even begin to wonder what happened. He may start to miss his princess, confused about why he decided to walk away. And if he has heard that another man may have entered the picture, this lights a fire under him like no other. Unbeknownst to you (the Love Addict), the Commitment Phobe can't live with you, and he can't live without you. His waffling and unhealthy thought processes cause him to make irrational decisions that he usually later regrets.

Convincing you he has changed due to desperation and fear, the Commitment Phobe may be relentless in his approach to renew this relationship and win back your love. But did he go get professional help? Work on his issues? Look in the mirror and take responsibility? No. He just woke up one day and missed you. But he isn't too strong-willed in his attempts to win you over. He dangles just enough carrot to get your stomach growling. And when you open your arms to welcome him back, the Commitment Phobe almost immediately turns in the other direction.

IT'S NOT PERSONAL

Was I too much of a nag? Was I too needy?

Did I not show him how much I loved him?

Was I too jealous?

Was I too controlling?

Was I too much of a pushover?

Yes, sort of, kind of and not at all. In other words, you drew the Commitment Phobe to you, and the end was predetermined. There is nothing you could have said, done, sucked or kissed that would have secured his place as the future Mr. Love Addict. The only way to sabotage this even further would have been by remaining a doormat.

Not taking rejection personally is obviously easier said than done and may sound impossible. But the truth of the matter is this breakup is not about you. It does not mean you are unworthy, imperfect, unlovable or unattractive. It has nothing to do with the car you drive, the clothes you wear, your height, your weight or your hair color. It's just that somewhere along the line, you have left this one man in charge of your self-esteem. He is not God, and you have to learn to take back your power. The idea that he no longer wants to be in the relationship with you only means that you have been spared.

The Commitment Phobe simply cannot commit, and this alone is the reason he left. He may have various justifications for why he moved on (temporarily anyway), but they are all based on fear and insecurities. There is a reason that this guy was resistant to change, outside help or introspection. He doesn't deal well with reality and was feeling the pressure of having to open his eyes.

HOPE AND DENIAL

With high hopes that everything will go back to the way it was in the *beginning*, we refuse to believe that the man from those days is actually gone. Denial is tricky, and we use it to preserve our sanity and avoid pain. We begin to believe that perhaps he is having a mid-life crisis before mid-life has even begun. Perhaps he lost our phone number, or his e-mail account was hacked. Or maybe he is having a mental breakdown and will call any minute professing what a mistake he made because some poltergeist entered his body and made this terrible breakup decision for him!

We secretly hope he will suffer without us and look forward to the day he comes crawling back on his knees—when we can finally have the last word and break up with *him*! We rationalize that we just want to regain the power one last time so that we can be the one to break it off once and for all.

Whether our denial runs deep or sneaks up on us from time to time, we have to recognize that this is the way we set ourselves up for failure. We avoid the truth by denying reality, but if we can grasp the Commitment Phobe's pattern early on, we can save ourselves a lot of heartache in our future relationships.

OBSESSIVE THINKING

At this point, we have called mom, dad, sister, cousin, therapist, neighbor and the state trooper all to figure out what in the world went wrong. We begin to wonder what he is doing and whom he is doing it with. We imagine that he is living this fruitful existence and reveling in his new-found freedom while we try to swallow down a few Cheerios in between tears. In our minds, he is immensely enjoying the world without us. The truth is that his life is not the incredible majestic wonder that we think it is. He's not lying in bed with five beautiful women being fed grapes. More likely, he is sitting around eating Cocoa Puffs and watching reality television and porn. If we have no idea what he is doing, there is no reason to torture ourselves with the worst when the worst is not even happening. There is always a choice, and we can choose differently.

Picture the Earth from outer space and see him from far, far away. When you start to see the bigger picture, he becomes very, very small and practically invisible. The only power he still has over your emotions is imaginary. In fact, it always was.

Look at the bright side, you don't have to wonder anymore what mood he will be in when you open the door, and you no longer have to guess what he is thinking 24 hours a day.

THE COMMITMENT PHOBE'S NEW SQUEEZE

The Commitment Phobe may have a plan B. Whether an ex or a newbie, he has high hopes that another woman will fill that empty void, even if just for a Saturday night rendezvous. After all, being alone is not the Commitment Phobe's pleasure. As mentioned earlier, it may happen that the Commitment Phobe will move on to his next relationship and leave the Love Addict wondering what she did that made this guy unable to commit to her. Twelve-step programs are the first to point out to never compare your insides with someone else's outsides. We have no idea what is going on in his new life, and it is neither our job nor any of our business to make his next relationship about our feelings. We have to stick to the issue at hand and worry about our own future and happiness by placing ourselves deep under the microscope, leaving him and his new friend (another Love Addict) to tend to their own weird science.

Unless the Commitment Phobe has had a major wake-up call, has tended to his feelings and dealt with his past, it is incredibly unlikely that he is living the good life with this new woman. Sooner or later, she will be reading this book while you are miles ahead of the game, having conquered your self-inflicting demons and realizing your own worth and value along the way.

HOLD, PLEASE

After everything was said and done, the Commitment Phobe would prefer if he could keep you on hold for future reference, sexual gratification or even another go at a relationship. While he cannot openly say these words, he can and will use code.

Texting, e-mailing, Facebook-stalking and checking in on you via a third party are ways in which the Commitment Phobe will attempt to keep tabs. Any means of connection gives him the much-needed assurance that you are still single and available when and if he should decide he wants to saddle that horse again. He may even tell you "someday" or "maybe one day" to get you to snap on that *hold tag* like a future department store purchase.

MY STORY

Length of Relationship: *One year and eight months.* **Commitment Phobic Attributes:** *Shut down, self-absorbed, fearful.*

When it comes to this push/pull relationship, I usually prefer telling my friends' and clients' stories. But I thought this was a good time to tell a story of one Commitment Phobe I had the pleasure of creating back in good old 1997.

I met Nick through an ex-boyfriend (red flag number one), and we became fast friends and even quicker lovers. I always did the calling, pursuing and detailing of our plans together. He didn't want to do much except watch his favorite sports team get slaughtered during Monday night football. And when he wasn't obsessing about that, he was betting on games and complaining about his mother. The attention and affection he showed me were fleeting, and what's worse, he would only have sex when it was his idea. He also took the liberty of kicking me out of his home whenever he wanted some space. He was a real gem. But I would rather have put up with this disrespect than be alone and have no one, right? So, I did what any Love Addict would do, and I stayed in the relationship while praying he would change.

After nearly two years with this guy, I was set up on a blind date and happily went behind Nick's back to meet this mystery man. Not surprisingly, I fell in love with my date at first sight, and Nick suddenly became an obstacle in my path toward true love. I went from completely obsessing over the same guy for nearly two years to obsessing about someone totally new. After the blind date, I called Nick the next day to tell him I wanted to break up, and that I had met someone I was interested in. Keep in mind, I was not angry at this point. It was almost like calling to change cable services. I actually felt a little bad for breaking the news, but I really didn't think he would care that much, and he responded accordingly.

About a week after the breakup, I got a call from Nick. To my surprise, he was inconsolable. He was sobbing and begging, and he told me he hadn't eaten in nearly a week. He said his parents and brother had been out to visit him because they were so worried. Needless to say, I was in complete shock. This guy was desperately distraught over *me*? He barely knew my last name and kicked me out of his house without blinking! I had spent two years waiting for this guy to express some kind of feeling toward me after the *beginning*, but this was extreme, and most of all, it simply made no sense.

I spent the next few weeks dividing my time between my new boyfriend (another Commitment Phobe) and bringing Nick soup because I felt terrible. There I was taking responsibility for his pain when he could not have cared less about mine during our relationship. This certainly was not a sign of a healthy thinker, I thought. Why didn't Nick know what he had when he had it? If I had gone back to him, the relationship would have eventually taken the same course. He did not see his own issues, nor did he suddenly realize how much he loved me; he had only woken up to his fears.

CHAPTER 15

Healing a Broken Heart

"With everything that has happened to you, you can either feel sorry for yourself or treat what has happened as a gift. Everything is either an opportunity to grow or an obstacle to keep you from growing. You get to choose."

- Wayne Dyer

The push/pull relationship may not always seem fair, but it is worth the ride if we can use it to The The push/pull relationship may not always seem fair, but it is worth the ride if we can use it to transform our inner lives. This includes encountering bumps on the road that may feel intense at the time. But with every feeling of rejection, frustration or abomination comes an opportunity to trust, look within and turn it around. It's in that trusting that we free ourselves to rely on our own self-love to overcome any outside forces that our ego believes can threaten our existence.

First of all, a healthy relationship requires that we are never dependent on the other person for our own self-worth. There is nobody outside of ourselves that can ever be responsible for our happiness. This may sound very depressing at first, but it can be a very empowering source of freedom. And having felt powerless for so long, this can be a major relief.

There is nothing wrong with feeling deep pain and deep loss. Not knowing who we are after the Commitment Phobe leaves, or having a feeling of emptiness is a sign that too much of our worth has been placed in one person's hands.

THE GIFT OF PAIN

Pain can be a powerful gateway to our happiness and growth. It is, therefore, important that we don't avoid, alter or ignore our pain. We should thank the Commitment Phobe for leaving this relationship and leaving us in such misery! Pain is the gift we receive when we are ready for a better life, a better option. If we have just been set free from this guy, we have a tremendous opportunity for growth. The worst mistake we make is avoiding pain because the only way out is *through*.

Often times, we keep attracting the same type of men over and over, and we never stop to sit with our pain to uncover what lies underneath and heal what is there. We likely avoided it by drinking, eating, smoking, watching television, dating or some other avoidance technique. But we cannot move past the lesson until we feel our pain fully and see it as an integral part of this experience. By avoiding and masking our feelings, we will keep reliving the past, time and again. We need to welcome the pain because there is power in it. It will lead us to a place inside that has been waiting a long time for us to show up.

BABY STEPS

Too often, you may try to tackle all of your problems in one day. Don't project the 100 things you need to do to change your life. You only need to do one thing at a time. In fact, doing more than one thing at a time would just assure that you don't give 100% to every task.

Figure out what you can do today to help yourself feel better. Perhaps you simply go for a walk. Maybe you write a letter to one of your parents, forgiving them for being human and letting you down. Make a list of what you want to do, what you have a passion for and start small. You can accomplish seven small steps in a week by simply spending an hour a day doing something that makes you happy. You have to retrain your brain to feel the chemistry of happiness and joy. And this does not happen overnight. Sometimes when you feel down and out, you might look at the giant task of "getting your life together" as this huge insurmountable list that seems so impossible to achieve that you just give up and turn on the TV. Your mantra is usually *I will get to it later*.

LINKING THE PAST

Feeling abandoned in the past *may* have contributed to the pain of this current rejection being so sharp. Children easily feel rejected, abandoned and unimportant at the slightest little thing, especially if the man who has their heart from the beginning, their father, is involved. Luckily, as an adult, you have a choice. Let go of the past and take notice that the pain over your recent relationship could be directly linked to past abandonment pain. It is not the Commitment Phobe who caused this unbearable pain. It may be the past that you have not yet healed or an inner fear of unworthiness and inadequacy. This last relationship could be an important catalyst for awakening.

THE BIRTH OF REJECTION

It's hard enough to feel happy, successful and thriving in this world with all that can go on, but when rejection is added to the equation, our self-esteem can take a big hit. But if we let our fears of rejection run our relationships and keep us from trusting and opening our hearts, we will never have the opportunity to truly love and be loved. Fear of rejection can be debilitating for many Love Addicts. And it can be a paralyzing predecessor for those of us who are unwilling to take the risk with emotional intimacy.

When the rejection we suffered from a previous breakup, parental neglect or devastating loss of life is so severe, it could potentially lead us to close off indefinitely, protecting ourselves from future pain. We create our own rejection because we are the creators of all things in our lives. If the current guy isn't the right fit, he will eventually move on. To experience an opposite truth, rejection can reveal a different face: a miracle in disguise.

Rejection is a part of all relationships, whether it is with partners, lovers, friends, children, bosses, pets or parents. Taking the risk of being rejected is scary, but we must risk rejection every day to find our strengths. Rejection, when viewed properly, is actually life's way of giving us what we want in the long run. Relationship success and failure are inevitable. But who is to say what is deemed a failure? Arguably, our greatest failures can become our biggest successes.

SELF DEFENSE

Too often, we let the past dictate our future and, in turn, start to shut down after a few bad experiences. After being burned by a Commitment Phobe, it's hard to let our defenses down and allow others in. But if we want a relationship with substance, we eventually need to set aside our personal agendas and take a look at the bigger picture. The more we let ourselves be open and susceptible to the unpredictable outside world, the more we allow the wonders of life in. A deep-seated fear of rejection can be so strong that some women are unable to maintain any intimate relationship whatsoever.

The Love Addict can sometimes move to the extreme, alienating anyone who seeks love and affection from her. Independence can be an overly abused and poorly used defense mechanism that keeps future relationships at arm's length. Some cease giving and receiving love altogether. If we live in fear that every date, relationship or marriage could end in a devastating and debilitating rejection, we must look into the past to find out where this belief system first originated.

THE MYTH OF TIME

The myth that time heals all wounds is exactly that: a myth. After the relationship with the Commitment Phobe has ended, you call up your friends, and they say, "You'll feel better in a few weeks. It just takes time." And on and on they go. The reality is that while their intentions are good, they are wrong.

Nothing heals on its own in time. But in time, you can heal yourself.

Taking care of yourself emotionally, spiritually and physically while enduring the pain of a breakup is of the utmost importance. Read books, write down your thoughts, go for a jog, mourn, figure out who you are and determine who you want to be. This is time for you and no one else. You cannot have a healthy relationship until you are happy with life and yourself. No one is out there that will complete you. You must be complete before you can attract a committable man.

To avoid making the same mistake twice, it's important to do the work to heal and finally become a whole individual. Find out how you drew in a man who abandoned you. Look at your past and search far and wide for answers. True, if you sit around and do nothing, go out with your friends and hit the bars or date a new guy, you will eventually forget about him. But what about *you*? What about the next guy you get involved with? Miraculously, you will inevitably end up with the same guy and the same circumstances in a different costume with a different address.

WORST-CASE SCENARIO

Dealing with the pain of loss can often leave the Love Addict with a less-than-ideal sense of the future. You fear, fret and worry that life may never get better. But if you can handle the worst-case scenario in your mind, you will feel much better about moving forward.

Let's pretend that the worst-case scenario is that you live alone, never find another man and order the Denny's breakfast special on Saturdays while chatting with the waitress regarding your recent bout with hemorrhoids. You frequent matinees, call your dad on weekend nights and listen to him talk about the failings of the current president. You house a few stray cats, buy a bus pass and play bingo on Mondays with your bird-watching group.

The best-case scenario is that you find yourself in the arms of a strong, confident and committable man who wants to give you the world. You both love to travel, watch *The Walking Dead* on Sundays, frequent the local flea markets, dream about having 2.5 children (You both despise the theory of carbon footprints.) and stay in bed together on Monday mornings.

Your perception is constantly changing as you grow. What you may want today may not be what you want five years down the line. There is no need to judge one life as good and the other as bad. Your perception is by far the most powerful tool you have. When you shift your perception, the worst-case scenario isn't all that bad after all. You won't have to do laundry for two or have fights over who is the better listener. *The Walking Dead* was never that good of a show. You can get ticks while traveling. Flea markets have a bunch of other people's used junk, while staying in bed all day is just plain lazy. And who wants half a child? And seriously, two eggs any style and a side of flapjacks does make a good meal. Hemorrhoids go away after time, unlike other pains in the ass, and your dad probably has a lot more political insight than you. Public transportation is good for the environment, while matinees mean no annoying moviegoers to contend with. Birds are pretty beautiful to look at, and let's just be honest, cats are much smarter than dogs. And you can actually win good money playing bingo.

RAIN'S STORY

Length of Relationship: *Five weeks.*

Commitment Phobic Attributes: *Deceitful, overly emotional, lying.*

When I think of extreme romances, I can't help but think of Rain and Josh. They met at a neighborhood bar and instantly hit it off. Both were from small towns and moved to the big city, had careers in music and loved the idea of opening their own bed-and-breakfast. Josh told Rain everything she ever wanted to hear...on the first night.

Over the next five weeks, they saw each other quite often, and he was very attentive. When he finally told her he wasn't ready for a relationship, not only was Rain hurt but she was also understandably confused because Josh was the one who kept referring to them in the future tense as a couple.

How could Rain have suffered a broken heart after only five weeks? When a Love Addict feels the pangs of abandonment, logic and reason are usually on vacation in the Greek Isles. Rain was a typical Love Addict, confusing commitment phobia with rejection. At the time, she didn't realize that the signs were all there: Josh was fast-moving, overly emotional, irresponsible, embellishing and talking "big" much too soon.

Spending her days in bed and feeling generally sorry for herself, it was hard for Rain to get over Josh. She remained hopeful that he was only temporarily spooked (which, of course, he was). However, a man who ups and leaves out of fear of committing will do it again. And Rain wasn't going to let that happen. She got a grip and decided to work on loving herself instead.

In the meantime, Rain wondered what she did to create this mess, and she began to take responsibility for her side of this fly-by-night affair. While some answers were coming to her with more ease, she still wished she could figure out what in the world he was really thinking.

CHAPTER 16

Commitment Phobic Types

"His problem is that he doesn't want anyone until he can have anyone he wants."
— Clifford Cohen, *Shots of Wit*

Two *main* types of Commitment Phobes are out there for the Love Addict to get her hands on, and neither is good for the relationship. While one knows that he never wants to commit, the other (and more common of the two) believes he is ready, willing and able to grab love by the horns.

The other Commitment Phobic types include women, married men, Don Juans, long-distance lovers, the quickie and the ever-so-popular dating site addicts. These types vary in intensity, but all have common fears. Each has similar characteristics with different ways to express their phobias. No matter what type the Commitment Phobe is, their behaviors are equally devastating to a Love Addict.

THE UNCONSCIOUS COMMITMENT PHOBE

It may come as no surprise at this point that the majority of Commitment Phobes are unaware that they have a problem. This guy truly believes that he wants marriage, commitment and lasting love. He has no idea that he is his own worst enemy, sabotaging anything good that comes his way. This guy does not know he has a fear-based problem. He categorizes himself as picky and unwilling to settle for less than the best. What he does not realize is that perfection is impossible, and while there are always other prospective love matches around the next corner, they are usually no better or worse than the woman he has right there in front of him.

The Commitment Phobe spends his time tossing and turning over whether or not he is making the right choice. But he never stops to realize that this is a habitual effort to avoid commitment. This type of Commitment Phobe can go years without a solid relationship because he does not want to make a mistake or end up in a relationship that he may not want in the end. His constant waffling makes it hard for him to see what he could have if only he could let go of the fear.

This type is usually honest in the *beginning* and truly believes that a connection has been made. He is not planning on chewing you up and spitting you out. The Commitment Phobe's intentions are real, but when the chase ends and the Love Addict sees him eye-to-eye, his fears are triggered and panic sets in, undermining his notion of true love. The unconscious Commitment Phobe is the most common...and the most deceptive. He is also the hardest to recognize.

THE CONSCIOUS COMMITMENT PHOBE

The conscious Commitment Phobe typically knows he is putting on an act in the *beginning*. He truly enjoys the woman he is pursuing but has no intention of staying with her until the bitter end. He would much rather play his odds and bet on the one who opens her legs first. This guy knows he is not fit to commit and would rather remain single and have his pick of the litter for the rest of his life.

Every so often, the conscious Commitment Phobe commits and tries to make it work. When he begins cheating or openly admitting his desires to get out of the relationship, the Love Addict is surprised. But the conscious Commitment Phobe can sometimes be honest about his fears, making him respectable. However, more often, the conscious type is looking for fun and is easy to spot by his extremely short-lived relationships or complete lack thereof. Sometimes the unconscious Commitment Phobe can become conscious by looking within and learning to commit.

THE MARRIED COMMITMENT PHOBE

By now, we understand (because we're so understanding) that the Commitment Phobe loves a challenge. Just like in the pre- beginning, he lives for the thrill of the chase. The unconscious Commitment Phobe actually wants to get married more than anything. Remember the alcoholic scenario? He wants to commit without infidelity, much like the alcoholic wants to quit drinking. But we all know that alcoholism requires inner work, Alcoholics Anonymous (AA) or some other means of massive introspection to cope with the disease. The Married Commitment Phobe does not even know he has a problem, let alone ask for help.

This particular gentleman is the one who cheats on his wife, perhaps joins a singles website, watches porn, ignores her pleas for affection and communication, shuts her out or generally has a hard time looking her in the eye. The Married Commitment Phobe feels that there must be an issue with his attraction toward his wife because he can't quite seem to figure out why he wants to sleep with the entire *Sports Illustrated* summer spread. Now, of course, what man would not want to hop in the sack with a gorgeous model wearing a dental floss bathing suit? The difference is that a committable man is grateful for what he has at home and feels completely confident in his choice of a wife mainly because of his confidence in decision-making. The committable man does not dwell on the past or search around corners for the bigger and better deal. He trusts himself and his decisions without squirming around in his insecurities and regrets. The committable man looks forward, not back.

The Married Commitment Phobe can drive his Love Addict wife up a wall for years with his pushing, pulling, cheating, shutting down and walling off. However, she is just as guilty in her addiction when she tolerates this horrible cruelty and teaches her children to tolerate more. But when the Love Addict cannot find her way out of this waning relationship due to financial or mental stressors , this duo can often be bound for life.

On the other side of the Married Commitment Phobe is the "other woman" who waits for him to leave his wife, sometimes for decades.

THE FEMALE COMMITMENT PHOBE

Every so often, a woman will be at the end of the Commitment Phobe spectrum, and her male partner will be at the end of the Love Addict spectrum, since this duo always attracts each other. A Female Commitment Phobe, like her male counterpart, is always seeking out new prey while the last carcass is still warm.

Facing extraordinary pressure from friends and family, some Female Commitment Phobes marry many times and have a hard time staying or leaving. Many of these women are business owners and committed solely to their personal success. They are only interested in relationships that don't tie them down or keep them from living their dreams. However, the Female Commitment Phobe may not realize that this is her way of escaping love and hence, possible rejection. She keeps her heart hidden under her sleeve, her head out of the sky and her feet firmly planted on the ground, avoiding anything too emotional.

THE LONG-DISTANCE
COMMITMENT PHOBE

The typical Commitment Phobe is pretty good at long-distance relationships. The most problematic of them enjoy having two lives: one with you and the other with someone else who may be reading this book. Never quite trusting his own inherent instincts and feelings, the Long-Distance Commitment Phobe has difficulty with decision-making. Therefore, he would rather have two lives in case one doesn't work out or he gets bored. The woman who is far away is usually the secondary character in this guy's love life. This dance can sometimes go on for quite some time without the Love Addict even knowing. These two rarely see each other, and the Love Addict gets her relationship oxygen from the Long-Distance Commitment Phobe's empty promises of visiting.

No matter what the promise, the Long-Distance Commitment Phobe does not have any intention of moving or having his partner move out in his direction. But, in the rare cases where the Love Addict does move in with the Long-Distance Commitment Phobe after being apart, it usually starts to fizzle just as she steps off the plane. The Commitment Phobe does not want to reveal too much about his other life, and combining these worlds can be disastrous. As much as he wants the Love Addict to be near him, he cannot help but sabotage the union once reunited.

It is important to keep in mind that not all long-distance relationships are between Commitment Phobes and Love Addicts. Many successful, happy couples have met far away from each other and have made it work until they could be together. But this book is not about them. This book is about our guy, the one who keeps us guessing at every turn.

THE ONLINE COMMITMENT PHOBE

This type may, by far, be the most disturbing. After months of coercion from your friends to "get out there" in the dating world, you reluctantly sign up on the hippest new dating site, create a profile page and upload your cutest photos, all the while gripping a bottle of wine. A few days later, some handsome lad pops up on your page, sends out a wink and sparks up a conversation. You immediately click on his profile:

Name: Melvin

Age: 32

Status: Single

I am a college graduate, and I am looking forward to opening my own company soon. I live just outside the city. I am a real guy looking for a real girl to settle down and share my life with. You must love dogs because my German shepherd, Charlie, can sense if you don't. LOL. I like sushi, playing guitar, long hikes, game night, watching Glee (guilty pleasure, I'm straight I swear!), cooking pasta and working out. (I am in great shape, but you will know that when you see me.) I just want to find my soul mate and travel the world. Maybe we are a match?

Willing to look past his name, the LOLs and the 20-mile drive, you wink back and send a note that reads: "I like dogs, as long as they don't bite, lol!"

You hit it off like gangbusters, and the first date is set for the following Wednesday. In the meantime, the texts get more and more flirtatious, and you are feeling like this could even possibly be it! But you play it cool and don't lose your perspective just yet. LOL.

Wednesday comes around, and you meet him at

the restaurant where he looks a little worse than his picture. But since you decided on the car ride over not to be judgmental, you let it slide. He is still cute, though, and the conversation flows... and flows...and flows. Is this for real? Five hours later and still laughing, you are already mentally testing out his last name after your first. A long kiss good night seals the deal, and he tells you he will call you tomorrow. You drive home, giggling all the way to your bedroom, and name your first child before drifting off into a dreamless sleep.

The next day, you awaken, singing songs from the musical *Annie* as you pour cream into your coffee. That day at work, you are on cloud nine as you feel the excitement over his impending phone call. But the day goes by and nothing. The week goes by and nothing. After a month, you pack up your imaginary children and catch the first flight off of Cloud Nine.

The truth is that while you may never know what really happened, you can be certain this guy was a Commitment Phobe. He could have been married, engaged, a masochist or a complete narcissist. Perhaps his deflating ego needed a boost. But the point is Commitment Phobes lurk everywhere, and until we change ourselves, heal our past and gain unconditional love for ourselves, we will continue to attract the Melvins of the world like magnets.

THE MULTI-PHOBE

The Multi-Phobe is like the Don Juan of Commitment Phobes, having a posse of women to choose from in case he gets bored. The Love Addicts who surround him usually have no idea about the others, unless this guy is bold enough to brag about his exploits. The Multi-Phobe is usually the one who never becomes "Facebook official" and keeps his online life hidden, sometimes having many profiles in the world of social media.

When a Love Addict discovers that she has been involved with this type, she usually convinces herself that what *they* had was real and the others were simply secondary characters in their big picture. The truth is that the Multi-Phobe has a "no discrimination" policy, and it's first come, first served. And when it comes to this guy, don't even dream of becoming official on Facebook. Many of these guys wouldn't know how to type those words without a mind-melting anxiety attack. Hiding the relationship from prospective lovers and exes is the top priority. He will simply lie about why he keeps his status a secret. He may say, "it's stupid" or "I don't want to hurt my ex's feelings." He enjoys all of his damsels equally, and having several of them keeps him safe from ever ending up alone. His grandiose nature and mysterious ways are typically the biggest signs that he is playing the field.

THE INSTANT COMMITMENT PHOBE

This guy is the one who is already mentally packing his bag right as he approaches you during last call. If we are aware, we can look back and see tiny snapshots of a faster-than-lightning affair off in the distance. This type of Commitment Phobe is like a bowl of sunshine. He is the one-night stand from the bar, the guy you talked to the entire night at your best friend's wedding or the handsome lad you made out with in the bathroom at the club on Saturday night. Okay, so some of this was your fault. But how were you to know this guy was full of shit when he whispered sweet nothings for hours? I guess his ridiculous dance moves, whiskey breath and pickup lines weren't clear enough clues.

This brief relationship happens fast, but he will

lie to get what he needs in a short period of time. Whether in a matter of hours, days or weeks, this type suddenly walks away, stops calling or ceases to exist without any notice. This is the guy who makes us wonder, *What happened to him? He seemed so interested! Why hasn't he called? Do you think he died?* He is a classic Instant Commitment Phobe. This type lacks total respect or empathy for others and women in general. With a larger than life ego, he is the biggest sweet talker of them all.

FREDERICK'S STORY

Length of Relationship: N/A

Commitment Phobic Attributes: *Conscious.*

Frederick is a friend of mine who openly admits he does not want to settle down. Ever. He is quite handsome and has many women approaching him at any given time. He enjoys sex, spontaneity and eternal freedom to be, do and choose what he wants at all times. He is open and honest with the women he meets and goes about his business without hurting anyone. He is not a bad guy for wanting to be single; he is a great guy for know-ing who he is and what he wants without hurting others in the process. If only all Commitment Phobes could be like Frederick. They would be much easier to spot.

Being a conscious Commitment Phobe has made Frederick an honest man. Right off the bat, he openly explains to his dates that he is not looking for a serious commitment—a respectable gesture. In turn, the women he dates can take it or leave it. If, after that point, they continue to see him and get hurt in the process, they only have themselves to blame. At that time, the Love Addict should take full responsibility for thinking that she will be the one to change him

CHAPTER 17

Inside the Mind of a Commitment Phobe

"To him who is in fear everything rustles."

- Sophocles

After everything is said and done, and done again and said, we are still unclear as to what is going on in his secretive mind that he keeps locked up and hidden behind a charming facade. No matter how hard we try to crack that code and get him to open up, figuring him out can still feel mind-numbingly impossible.

After the Love Addict's many attempts at intimacy, the Commitment Phobe begins to feel the pressure of committing. Words like "forever" and "eternity" cause fear to course through his veins, moving him to create an alternate life. The Commitment Phobe knows he is pulling away, and this confuses him. He thinks that these feelings mean he should make a different choice for a life partner. He begins to see his waning interest as a sign that he should be looking around the corner in case a better option comes along. Living with a Love Addict can be grueling at best. When we are addicted to love, our happiness is based on anything and everything the Commitment Phobe says or does, making him feel that he must be on point at all times.

The Commitment Phobe lives in a constant state of self-doubt and *what-ifs*. He may appear calm, cool, overly confident and collected, but once he reaches the nine-month threshold (if he has made it that far), his inner alarm clock begins to scream that there are more women out there better than his current squeeze. What he does not realize is that it's not the relationship that has the problem. Rather, it's his illusion that there is a perfect woman out there with a perfect halo over her head, parting the red seas with her majestic smile. Planning an escape route or shutting out the Love Addict becomes par for this relationship's rocky course.

The Commitment Phobe has a long list of things to do in his free time, including making sure his life is perfect before being in a committed relationship. Calling his exes, avoiding intimacy and working until the wee hours of the night can sometimes be at the top of that long list, as well. The Commitment Phobe often convinces himself that he should get his life together first before entering into a relationship, even though he is 45 years old and has a career, a condo and a vacation home in Switzerland.

Generally, with an unhappy internal life, the Commitment Phobe may struggle with bouts of depression, hiding from the outside world. Nonetheless, the confidence of a Commitment Phobe can appear unusually strong and convincing, working overtime to cover for his deep-seated insecurities. Inside his mind, he is questioning many of his decisions, lacking a great deal of trust in his choices, including women. Understanding the true feelings of a Commitment Phobe is nearly impossible, as getting into his mind could require a sledgehammer.

THE COMMITMENT PHOBE'S DENIAL

The Commitment Phobe believes that he genuinely wants to commit, much like an alcoholic wants to quit drinking. But imagine not even having the slightest clue that you are an alcoholic or that you even have a drinking problem. Instead, you blame the bottle. In this case, the bottle is the Love Addict. The Commitment Phobe usually wants to have children and live out his life with love and comfort. But for this guy, the impossible task of finding the perfect girl makes this push/pull relationship a never-ending struggle of *is she or isn't she The One*?

The constant denial of owning up to his side of this relationship dysfunction keeps the Commitment Phobe safe from guilt, responsibility and pain. He will be the first one to say he is looking for love and simply hasn't found the right one.

HIDDEN FEELINGS

As I mentioned earlier , the Commitment Phobe has great difficulty confronting his own inner demons and taking responsibility. He has an even harder time feeling his own feelings and owning up to the past. This is why, when driven to the brink, the Commitment Phobe either completely shuts down or cries like a confused child. The more issues in this man's past that he has avoided along the way, the more he wants to hide out in the hopes that you don't see inside of him. This Commitment Phobe simply may have a difficult time revealing his inner feelings because some-where along the line, his feelings were stifled or deemed inappropriate or wrong by his parents or authority figures. Like many young boys, he learned early on not to express his emotions.

Pushing his feelings down is the precise reason the Commitment Phobe cannot express himself to the Love Addict. It's not that he does not love her or feel strongly toward her. The Commit-ment Phobe's inability to properly communicate stems from his own fears and insecurities, creat-ing a powerful divide with the Love Addict, who sometimes works overtime to get him to open up. And when her attempts fall short, she ques-tions what went wrong.

Oftentimes the Commitment Phobe's feelings are quite off-balance. He may pour his heart out to the Love Addict in times of comfort, telling her how much he loves her and never wants to lose her. He is genuinely giving her an achingly painful glimpse inside his confused mind. But when the next day rolls around, he closes up like a clam. This extreme emotional scale the Com-mitment Phobe jumps around on is not healthy. Confessing his love for the Love Addict one week and shutting down the next are not indicative of clarity and balance.

Aside from sadness and pain, anger can often lurk within the complicated mind of the Commitment Phobe. This is just another emotion that leaks out through the cracks after feelings of the past and present have been suppressed. Ready to explode, the Commitment Phobe can often be like a ticking time bomb, never giving notice as to what could set him off.

Even committable men have difficulty expressing feelings.

Therefore, this is not a distinguishing characteristic of commitment phobia. However, when it comes to feelings, the more intense, painful and passionate the relationship with the Love Addict is, the more this duo thinks it must be love!

ME, ME, ME

A confident, healthy, self-loving man is not only capable of taking care of himself but others, too. The Commitment Phobe has a much higher tendency to be self-absorbed. This self-absorption is the opposite of self-love. He comes off as self-absorbed because he works tirelessly to keep himself safe from his feelings and the opinions and judgments of others. In other words, he uses his ego as protection.

Self-Absorbed: *What will they think of what I look like? Will others see me as successful? What can I do to help myself be happier? What if I get hurt?*

Self-Love: *I like who I am and what I look like. I hope others find success. I want to help that person be happier. I don't want to hurt anyone.*

The men with self-love is ready and willing to take on the feelings of others and is secure enough to seek out opportunities to help others. These guys are usually the ones asking, "How are you?" The self-absorbed men are usually the responders in this case. They make it all about themselves, create a selfish annotation to their personas and sometimes seek the center of attention. In actuality, it is insecurity and fear seeping through their shaky façade.

The Commitment Phobe may be the first person to call the Love Addict a drama queen, but this guy attracts more drama than a cast of characters on a soap opera. His ego feeds on drama and needs it to survive, giving him fuel for the fire.

Whether it's the chaos he causes in his own life or his "crazy" ex, he seems to always be the common denominator.

SHAME AND GUILT

We now know about the Commitment Phobe's hidden feelings of inadequacy. Many of them do not feel deserving of love, and they may even question why the Love Addict is wasting her time with him. His fears and insecurities can keep love out and make it near impossible for any woman to be there for him.

At the end of the day (a long and suffocating day), the Commitment Phobe may even feel guilty and know he was wrong. But this realization doesn't exactly make him blurt out his heartfelt apology or recite a love poem. He would rather stuff that feeling down with the rest of them and pretend it all never happened. After mistreating the Love Addict time and again, the Commitment Phobe *can* feel sorry. But eventually, he begins to question why she would stick around to tolerate him, putting her self-esteem into question.

THE PERFECT WOMAN

In the eyes of many Commitment Phobes, you

were initially perfection personified. Your glowing confidence, inner strength and cool-girl persona grabbed the Commitment Phobe's attention quite early in the game. This, of course, was all before he subconsciously turned you into an obsessive, jealous, withering, insecure, crazy control freak (but kept it all inside, of course).

His main squeeze is suddenly no longer The One, and the Commitment Phobe's quest to find the perfect girl marches on as he thinks a more perfect woman and singing angels could be right around the corner. But the Commitment Phobe also remembers the *beginning* of the relationship and, therefore, constantly questions whether or not you could be it. This is the reason he may go back and forth until someone eventually calls it quits.

ANXIETY AND FEAR

Since the Commitment Phobe has a hard time trusting his own feelings, he often wonders if he has made the right choice.

Whether it's women, cars, homes or a trip to the movies, the Commitment Phobe can often vacillate over every decision. Since he is looking for the perfect woman, he questions if he has found her at every turn. And because the perfect woman does not exist, the Commitment Phobe ends up alone and feeling anxiety over never getting it right.

The stress that the Commitment Phobe struggles with can come from a variety of sources: fear of intimacy, fear of marriage, fear of being a good provider, fear of enmeshment, fear of rejection, fear of losing his freedom, fear of fatherhood, fear of cohabiting or fear of being a family. Any or all of these can give the Commitment Phobe anxiety.

As time marches on within this relationship, the Commitment Phobe may feel a sense of impending doom when his freedom is being threatened. He wants to hold on to his space but feels swallowed up by his surroundings. And, for the Commitment Phobe, the idea of having sex with only one woman forever is enough to make him cry. Whatever would he do with all of the potentially available exes, neighbors, coworkers, playmates and movie stars in his head?

Seeing marriage as a freedom killer, the Commitment Phobe may fear he will have to give up his identity to become Mr. Committed. The less obligation, the better. No matter how much

Inside the Mind of a Commitment Phobe

space the Love Addict offers him, the Commitment Phobe is thoroughly convinced that he will have to give up his oxygen to be with her. Life as he once knew it would be over.

Since the Commitment Phobe is far more insecure than we may realize, the threat of losing his King of the Jungle status can be paralyzing. Hence, the fear of losing his masculinity is at the forefront of his mind. He truly wants to be emotionally close to the Love Addict, he just doesn't see that he can have his identity and still have love. He does not see that commitment is a strength and not a weakness.

BOUNDARIES

The Commitment Phobe is a man of few words and has a very difficult time expressing his feelings. But when he does, they pour out, creating an imbalance of emotions. He is either shutdown or wide open.

Some internal feelings of inadequacy can keep the Commitment Phobe from opening up. He has his boundaries in the form of walls, and, after some time, we realize that even the chisels of love and support cannot tear it down. Often, the Commitment Phobe fears that someone may see through these walls straight into who he is. He has his guard up, worrying about exposure and may go to great lengths to assure his safety. By using walls, the Commitment Phobe is kept safe from harm, judgment, suffocation and, unfortunately, love.

When putting up walls, the Commitment Phobe shuts out the Love Addict, who may not be smothering him whatsoever. The problem may be all in his head, but there is nothing the Love Addict can do to change his perception. The Love Addict may genuinely be giving him enough space to launch a rocket ship, but he feels suffocated nonetheless.

Due to these poor boundaries, the Commitment Phobe fears he could be swallowed up by the emotions of the Love Addict, overwhelming him to the point that he runs. Closed is better, he concurs. That is, until a woman disguised as perfection walks into his life.

To have a healthy relationship, boundaries must be present. Healthy boundaries would help the Commitment Phobe to not feel enmeshed by the Love Addict or in charge of her feelings. Taking on the responsibility of his partner's every emotion can be a debilitating feeling for the Commitment Phobe. He doesn't realize that he is not the gatekeeper of the Love Addict's feelings of sadness, happiness, anger and fear. He may think this is part of his "job," and the pressure can feel like a million tons. Due to poor boundaries, exchanging feelings between the Commitment Phobe and the Love Addict can lead to major problems in communication, misunderstandings, drama and the ultimate demise of the relationship.

SECRETS, SECRETS

The Commitment Phobe appears as one big mystery toward the middle and end of the relationship. His Jekyll and Hyde persona is making its debut, and you can't quite figure out who is behind which curtain. Being an open book is the last thing the Commitment Phobe wants. He is quite content living two lives until he decides which one he wants to sign a permanent contract with.

With an obvious veil of secrets, and possibly hiding behind a wall of indiscretions, the Commitment Phobe does not want to be found out. While he may appear to be quite a loner at times, the Commitment Phobe does not like being alone. While he would much rather be in the company of an iPhone, video game, work, pornography, bars, drugs or other women, he feels guilty doing so. Nonetheless, he will do anything to distract himself from looking within and dealing with any unwanted feelings.

Feeling the disconnect, it is quite easy for the Love Addict to take the secretive nature of a Commitment Phobe personally. Little does she know that his deep, dark well of secrets has nothing to do with her and everything to do with how he feels about himself.

DEREK'S STORY

Length of Relationship: *Nine months.*

Commitment Phobic Attributes: *Indecisive, workaholic, anxious, fearful.*

Understanding that he was a Commitment Phobe, Derek was at a standstill about leaving his girlfriend, Shawna. During one of our sessions, I recall telling Derek that love is as much a decision as it is something that comes over you. It is much like the way a woman gets pregnant by choice, and at the same time, pregnancy is something that is happening *to* her. I explained to him that a bright light was not going to illuminate the perfect woman, and that he would have to choose her just as much as she chose him. Of course, Derek wanted connection, passion, mutual respect, loyalty and honesty in a long-term commitment. He just could not decide whether he wanted to keep seeing Shawna, even though he fell in love with her in the *beginning*, and she had all of those aforementioned qualities. "What is Shawna missing that you are looking for?" I asked.

"I don't know. Nothing, I guess. I just felt so strongly about her in the *beginning* of our relationship, but somehow those feelings have changed, and I don't feel as excited anymore," he replied.

Derek learned that the Honeymoon Phase always ends, and that a relationship requires effort. After explaining this, Derek responded, "We don't have many problems, and I'm trying to put the work in, but I don't have time to hold her hand through our issues."

"Then let her go and find a willing partner," I suggested.

Derek stayed with Shawna another year before breaking up with her. By that time, Shawna was even more invested in the relationship. Furious that he had wasted her time, Shawna stormed out of Derek's life and went on to heal her own abandonment issues. Three weeks after living with regret and fumbling over his emotions, Derek was suddenly desperate to get Shawna back. She, however, discovered who she was and what she wanted...and it wasn't Derek.

CHAPTER 18

Why He Can't Commit

"Since the mind is conditioned by the past, you are then forced to reenact the past again and again."
- Eckhart Tolle, *A New Earth*

After better understanding his fears of intimacy, it is easier to see why the Commitment Phobe acts irrationally when it comes to love. While each Commitment Phobe is distinguishable on his own and has his own personality, there are certain definitive attributes in his emotional makeup.

Men who can't commit do not all share the same childhood experiences, nor have they necessarily lived similar lives. In fact, while one Commitment Phobe may have had loving parents who spoiled him, another may have never even known his parents. The Commitment Phobe can be rich, poor, kind, unkind, quiet or loud. These vast differences make figuring out why he fears commitment that much more difficult.

What leads him to be this way is still a mystery, but there are a few theories that can explain why he simply can't commit. Without introspection and healing, a dysfunctional childhood can often lead to a dysfunctional adulthood. Healthy thinking can take a back seat, and when all else fails, we blame our parents.

CHILDHOOD TRAUMA

For generations, children have been taught to be seen and not heard. Little girls should not show anger or strength, and young boys should not cry or show weakness. Boys were told to be strong and self-sufficient. Having been discouraged from talking about their feelings, these young boys grow up learning to shut down when an emotion other than anger or happiness emerges. Many of these boys did not learn how to communicate or understand their feelings, and as adults, they would rather bolt than find themselves in a deep discussion about their relationship.

Divorce can trigger abandonment in a young child, and if the father abandoned his family altogether, there are even more reasons the child could become an adult Commitment Phobe. His subconscious fear of being abandoned could lead him to ruin any future relationships, beating his Love Addict partners to the punch.

PARENTAL IMPACT

His father may have abandoned the Commitment Phobe, either emotionally or physically. His father may have been a workaholic or a Commitment Phobe himself, providing his son with an innate fear of abandonment, coupled with shame in expressing his feelings. This is one theory on why some of these men can't commit.

If his father is also a Commitment Phobe, he would likely be emotionally or physically in and out of his son's life. Perhaps his father had affairs, was emotionally abusive, an alcoholic or denied affection to the Commitment Phobe and his mother.

This type of upbringing could either lead the victim to be afraid of commitment or even become a Love Addict. But because men are wired in such a way that they are less emotional, they are more likely to be the noncommittal one.

By nature, men are simply less nurturing than women and many times don't understand the important role they play in their son's lives. Because fathers are taught throughout time not to show their emotions, unfortunately, that leads to issues with their own children. Women and men deal with their abandonment issues differently, which is why men pull away and women push toward.

While we're on a roll blaming family members, we can't forget about another innocent party to this guy's selfish adult life, his mother. The Commitment Phobe may have felt enmeshed with his mother because women are naturally nurturers and caretakers. When the mother is a Love Addict married to a Commitment Phobe herself, the child can feel stress. The mother may end up relying on her son for that love, enmeshing him and unwittingly making him responsible for her happiness. As an adult, the Commitment Phobe can sometimes fear women who seek to tie him down. However, this is not a common reason why men can't commit.

RELATIONSHIP PERFECTION

Some Commitment Phobes watched their parents frolic in Relationship Heaven. With parents who always showed each other love, respect, honesty and affection, sometimes the Commitment Phobe set his standards based on what he saw. As a child, the Commitment Phobe was not present for the arguments and issues his parents sometimes had behind closed doors. He only knew that perfect love, and he would never settle for less.

If the Commitment Phobe has seemingly perfect parental figures, his search for perfection may never end. Instead of looking for the right match for him, he will perpetually seek out perfection instead. The Commitment Phobe does not see that the right one for him *does* make her the perfect match. There is no perfect woman just as there is no perfect man, but there *is* such a thing as a perfect match.

If you want to know about the Commitment Phobe in your life, just ask his exes. When it comes to perfection, he didn't find it before you, and he is not going to find it after you. This guy does not know that perfection is an illusion and that the Honeymoon Phase can't last forever. As soon as the humdrum sets in, the Commitment Phobe sees imperfection in his partner, raising a red flag much too soon. With unrealistic expectations, the Commitment Phobe sets himself up for disappointment.

EMOTIONAL IMMATURITY

When it comes to maturity, the Commitment Phobe may be stuck in the past. Often with arrested development, he may even believe that he is ageless while beckoning young women out of his league. His inappropriate age identity keeps him trapped in a time warp. He never quite feels like an adult living in the real adult world. Things just don't feel normal for the Commitment Phobe, and he can't exactly pinpoint the reasons.

Never having had the opportunity to delve into his feelings as a child, he doesn't feel adequate as an adult, sometimes with the emotions of a teenager. This often makes the Commitment Phobe turn to substances, depression or other women that will temporarily numb his confusion. Growing up can be last on this guy's "to do" list.

THE EX FACTOR

The Commitment Phobe sees his exes as equal opportunity employers. He also sees them as crazy but has a hard time letting go of them. Much in the same way, he has a hard time letting go of you. It's important to him that he keeps the door cracked open to the past if he changes his mind or feels he made the wrong choice.

The Commitment Phobe will usually blame the downfall of his past relationships on his ex (another Love Addict) and tell you how crazy she made him, never quite taking responsibility for his push-pull antics and nightmarish behavior. He is banking on the fact that you will never actually *talk* to his ex. Being burned in the past by an ex can lead the Commitment Phobe down a path of victimization. He may even use her as a scapegoat to convince you that he is damaged goods.

This can be tricky because a Commitment Phobe may have had his heart broken in the past and will use this as an excuse to not open up. Many Commitment Phobes like to make it appear as if the last woman ruined him to deflect responsibility. Yes, his ex may have cheated on him, and he may truly have felt betrayed by her. However, using this as an excuse to refuse to move on or accept help is just another cop-out. If the Commitment Phobe has a broken heart, he likely brought it on himself, pushing his former Love Addict to the brink and forcing her to resign from the game. In essence, they are playing out their roles and are both equally responsible for the demise of the relationship.

LIFE ON THE FENCE

At this point, it comes as no surprise that this guy's issues run far beyond the usual hemming and hawing when it comes to decision making. By now, you understand that the Commitment Phobe's waffling can cause him anxiety and stress. But none so much as when he realizes that he has made a mistake. Because he can't commit to staying, and he can't commit to leaving, he sits uncomfortably on the fence waiting to be pushed. This is where he spends the majority of his life, never quite touching ground on either side.

The Commitment Phobe generally cannot commit to most things in his life. Purchasing a home, buying a car, taking a vacation or simply choosing a restaurant are all things that can cause waves of indecisiveness for this guy. The Commitment Phobe is always afraid of making the wrong decision, fearing that a better house, car, trip or restaurant could be right around the next corner, so he vacillates until the decision basically chooses him. This outlook on life can render the Commitment Phobe virtually powerless in his mind. He does not believe that he has the power to choose, create and live his own unique life. He

Why He Can't Commit 219

lets life make his choices for him by deciding not to decide much of the time.

THE BACKUP ARTIST

After just a short time of "you and he" togetherness, the Commitment Phobe starts to feel the heat, even if he lives in Alaska. This guy, similar to the Multi-Phobe, starts looking around the corner for the next best thing, never quite satisfied with his own choices. Just as he cannot let go of his exes, the Commitment Phobe believes the more, the merrier. He wants his cake and would like to eat it, too. All of it, from the soft, creamy middle to the fluffy, buttery layers, proving once again that the Commitment Phobe cannot leave the Love Addict unless he has one or two more on the side. *Women*, not cakes. Flirtatious encounters with other women make the Commitment Phobe feel at ease. His balancing act of two women is needed for the Commitment Phobe to let down his guard. He feels there is safety in numbers.

If the Commitment Phobe has left the relationship, he has someone else to go to, whether real or fictionalized. This other woman may simply be just another chase, a fun little escapade for him to focus on. The Commitment Phobe did not leave because he found the love of his life, but rather a new thrill that captured his attention. If you have just broken up with a Commitment Phobe, don't fret because this guy is not about to fall in love with the next woman who comes along and trot off into the sunset. Beware because he may come trotting back to you.

HANNAH'S STORY

Length of Relationship: *One year and one month.*
Commitment Phobic Attributes: *Angry, shut down, deflecting, blaming.*

Hannah's boyfriend, Matt, was the product of an alcoholic father. Instead of playing hide-and-seek with the neighborhood kids, his childhood was consumed with fear, shame and abuse. He watched his father come home drunk, and Matt saw his mother cry and scream at him for continually abandoning the family for other women. Matt became afraid of love because it seemed only to cause pain. As an adult, he had not sought therapy for his past emotional trauma, figured he was fine and moved on.

Before he met Hannah, Matt had a few relationships that were very brief, fearing he would become his father. This was by far his most serious concern, and he was smitten right off the bat. After some time, Matt began to spend less and less time with Hannah, shutting down frequently and refusing to talk about what was bothering him. Internally, Matt was conflicted, bouncing back and forth between feelings of inadequacy and superiority. When he was feeling insecure, he would often cozy up to Hannah, telling her how much she meant to him, usually right before making love. He would sometimes sob uncontrollably, admitting to his confusion about his love for her. Although few and far between, Hannah lived for these moments of deep connection.

Like most of her relationships, Hannah was fully committed to Matt even after she became aware of his commitment issues, but she made the decision to stand by him no matter what. After all, she understood him because she, too, was a victim of childhood neglect and certainly was not going to be the one to reinjure him. But not only was Matt uninterested in getting help but he also still blamed Hannah for their relationship problems.

The relationship came with a price for Hannah, who had eventually lost herself, along with her joy. She was the willing martyr, and Matt was her pet project. She was determined to get Matt healthy because, if she could just get him to love her, then she would finally be worth something.

CHAPTER 19

Can He Change?

"In our relationships, how much can we allow them to become new, and how much do we cling to what they used to be yesterday?"

\- Ram Dass

If you are eagerly reading this chapter and anxious to hear if the Commitment Phobe can change, then you are still in the throes of the push/pull trap. You are hoping beyond hope that he is capable of change. But will he? The short answer to this nagging question is *outlook not so good*.

However, a willing man is a changeable man, and where there is hope, there is a possibility. Willing does not mean pushing him into change. After all, forcing someone to love and respect you is a recipe for disaster. The Commitment Phobe wants love, and he looks for it in every Love Addict he finds. Both parties are wanting to soak up the love from the other, often never realizing that they are not loving one another in a healthy way. As both offending characters lack self-love in some way, they have a hard time giving away what they don't have, and they can easily mistake love for need.

REQUIREMENTS FOR CHANGE

Because the Love Addict often worries that her precious time has been wasted, she may feel it would be easier to change the man she's got rather than look for a new one. But the never-ending desire to change our husbands, boyfriends and lovers into knights, kings and princes is an age-old idealism that has yet to be proven fruitful . Change requires great introspection, desire and accountability. If the Commitment Phobe recognizes that he has a problem in regard to committing, then there could be a future for this duo.

Never fight with reality. And never try and change a Commitment Phobe. Waiting for a person to change is like waiting for politics to become honest. To change, he must first become *conscious* that he has a problem. But with acceptance of who he is, you can sometimes notice small changes in his behavior and big changes down the road if his intent is authentic and steadfast. Nonetheless, we can only change the one thing we ever had any control over to begin with—ourselves.

FIXING AN OLD CAR

Trying to change a Commitment Phobe is like banging your head against a wall while flying a plane and eating sushi. In other words, it does more damage than good. You are not able to change other people, and for some of you, this is bittersweet wisdom. But you can change your choices, and that can be very empowering.

Let's say you owned an old, broken, run-down 1982 VW Beetle that has been sitting in the garage for several months after having been smashed in an accident, crushed in the junkyard and robbed of its engine. But that little car was great when you first bought it! It was shiny, had a brand-new transmission and drove like a dream. And with only a few miles on the odometer, you loved this fancy little bug and took it everywhere.

Now, when you sit in that crappy car, it's still comfortable. You are so used to it that you can't imagine getting a new one, even if that new one were better and worked! These days, the little bug is not drivable, can't hold oil and falls apart even more when you try to start it. Plus, you wouldn't want to lose it to another driver because another driver may be smart enough and good enough to know just how to fix it up, and that would just make you jealous.

The path to purchasing a new car is actually much easier. You just mourn the old one and spend some time on public transportation with your favorite gal (that's you). Then figure out exactly what kind of car you want next before hopping into any old car that comes your way. This is much easier than dealing with all of the mechanical problems of the old one.

Especially with the cost of transmissions. Your love alone will not fix the car, and your love for him will not make the Commitment Phobe transform.

THE THERAPIST

With proper understanding and self-analysis, the Commitment Phobe is surely capable of change. However, I am not referring to the kind of change that happens when he gets help because you have taken it upon yourself to "fix" him, seeking out the perfect couples therapist where all he has to do is go for an hour to see if he likes it.

On top of that, the issue with forcing a man into therapy is twofold. Firstly, men hate being told they are doing something wrong. They want to feel like you admire and accept them for who they are. Don't worry, you did not "ruin" the relationship by trying desperately to get him into therapy. The relationship was in ruins far before this last-ditch effort.

Secondly, the Commitment Phobe really does not want to change because he is unconscious of his inability to commit. In fact, he thinks all the problems in the relationship stem from you! Why in the world would *he* go to therapy? He may go for no other reason than to appease or pass the blame on to you. In truth, the Love Addict is responsible for her half of the puzzle. A good therapist will point out the recurrent low self-esteem issue with you. The Commitment Phobe may also use means of a third-party therapist as a "way out" of the relationship. This way he won't look like the bad guy, and it will appear to others as if he did everything he could to fix this problematic relationship. This can be another clear indicator of the Commitment Phobe's deep denial.

THE LOVE ADDICT THERAPIST

With all your vast knowledge of the Commitment Phobe's issues, you are certainly equipped to handle a little love intervention with your sweetie, right?

Wrong.

We are convinced that if anyone can fix and change this guy, it's us. And if he really loved us, he would work on changing. We almost always try and drag him into therapy in the hopes that the professional will give it to him good. But just in case Dr. Phil is on vacation, we have a foolproof backup plan. We can *teach* him the way.

Unfortunately, your love cannot change him, nor can your therapeutic skills and willingness to tolerate his wishy-washy behavior. Many Love Addicts spend half their lives being the sacrificial lamb in this crazy twosome. But the truth is you are not his mother, and it is not your job to teach and enlighten the Commitment Phobe. If you are looking to get him help (and he is willing on his own terms to do so), there is hope for this relationship. But this must be *his* desire, not yours. The Commitment Phobe can change, but he has to be *all* in.

It is not the Love Addict's job to single-handedly improve the health of the relationship, nor is it possible. If he is willing to let go of his old beliefs and seek out help, then you can choose to join him on that journey. Just be mindful that you are your number one priority, and you were not put on this Earth to be his caretaker and show him the way. Attempting to change the Commitment Phobe without his awareness and consent is only a recipe for further discontent.

When I first completed an early edition of this very book, I gave it to a good friend who needed some love addiction intervention. About a week after I had given it to her, she forced her Commitment Phobe boyfriend to read it, too! In fact, they began reading it out loud to each other, and my friend was convinced it was *really* working. A month after her attempt to "fix" him, he walked out on her, pulling a Houdini to boot.

DID HE EVER LOVE ME?

After the Love Addict has thoroughly understood what has happened within the relationship and who the Commitment Phobe really is, she frequently wonders, *Was it even real?*

I have sat with Commitment Phobes in my office (usually they are dragged in), and these guys do feel remorse, many of them anyway. They know that their behavior is causing emotional harm to the Love Addict, but they just don't know how to stop it.

The important thing to know here is that the conscious Commitment Phobe does know that he is setting you up for failure. Whereas, most of the unconscious ones are unaware what they are doing to you until they know they want out but continue the relationship anyway. I said this would be tricky, so try and stay with me here.

The majority of the unconscious Commitment Phobes are looking for love and marriage. As I mentioned earlier in the book, they genuinely want these things and want the happily ever after with the woman of their dreams (too bad this woman only exists on paper). The ones with an honest intention in the *beginning*, however, do turn into conscious liars. Eventually, they pull the same rabbit out of the hat that worked so well in the *beginning*, knowing full well they do not mean it. But they need love, and they need to keep you around. The once unconscious Commitment

Phobe becomes aware that he is leading you on, but your feelings don't much matter to him because he is looking out for his own needs. To top that off, he is incapable of loving you in a healthy way. It is not because you are unlovable, it is simply because he lacks a certain amount of love and respect for himself.

INABILITY TO LOVE

The Commitment Phobe wants love more than anything. More than money, fame, success, family or material goods. But to get it from another person, he must first find it for himself. And if the Commitment Phobe loved himself, he would be aware of his personal integrity, take a careful self-inventory, keep his word, do his best no matter the task and take care of his body, mind and spirit. The Commitment Phobe is easily down in the dumps, sometimes self-loathing and critical of his failures and defeats and spends much of his free time in self-judgment and regret. In this way, the Commitment Phobe is sometimes too self-absorbed to deal with anyone other than himself.

Many Love Addicts have wondered why the Commitment Phobe would ever have tried at all to force himself into a relationship just to run away. The truth is that his fears have nothing to do with his feelings for the Love Addict. They are two separate entities in one way, and in another, they are directly related when it comes to his fear of making the wrong choice.

THE 80/20 SCENARIO

Some simple scenarios can help you gain perspective on your relationship if you are just willing to be honest. If your relationship is 80% good and 20% irritating, you are in good company. If 80% of the time, your relationship is dysfunctional and unhappy, and 20% of the time, it's great, you are settling for less. The Love Addict will often take that 20% to the bank and keep it there for safekeeping. She and the Commitment Phobe live for that 20%, making the 80% somewhat bearable. When this relationship is bad, it's heartbreaking, and when it's great, it's amazing.

The 80/20 scenario can be a good indicator of where the relationship is and where it's headed. But it's really a matter of where the numbers lie and what side has the majority. The push/pull relationship between the Commitment Phobe and the Love Addict is typically 80/20 on the negative turn.

To add insult to injury, if that 20% labeled "amazing" lacks the important ingredients such as communication, respect, support, understanding, honesty and trust, this could be even more problematic. These are fundamental relationship musts for any couple interested in commitment and longevity.

SETTLING

Settling for an unhappy relationship has become an art form for some of us, but what if we knew with certainty that real love was right around the corner, and all we had to do was love ourselves and trust that our love would be matched? It's easier said than done, like most things in life. But many Love Addicts are afraid of losing what they have for fear that they may end up with nothing. The truth is that having nothing may be better than our current situation. The only perfect relationship that exists is the one we have with ourselves, and outside of that, we all deserve true love and happiness. Settling for whatever randomness comes our way is not an option.

If we continually find ourselves sitting outside a big fishbowl, peering in on the happy and healthy relationships of our friends and family members, then it may be time to reassess our relationship. If we are constantly admiring other couples or comparing ourselves and coming out on the bottom each and every time, we may want to deal with our reality. Envy is an unnecessary evil.

It's not very often that we hear the jubilant announcement of true love...a perfect match that lasts beyond eternity. In fact, these instances are so rare they are usually referred to as "love stories." When such stories become reality, we wonder what went right, and we begin to speculate how those lovebirds got so lucky. Every relationship has holes in its infrastructure, imperfections, conflicting ideas and annoying idiosyncrasies.

Yet, for a couple to coexist, there must be compromise. To which degree we are willing to compromise is what separates the *settlers* from the *happily ever afters*?

Compromising on where to go on vacation is very different than compromising on daily happiness. Often the Love Addict is so afraid to lose the Commitment Phobe that she will settle for anything. After all, she understands him!

DIANE'S STORY

Length of Relationship: *Three years and three months.*

Commitment Phobic Attributes: *Cheating, deceiving, fearful, indecisive.*

Diane and Pete were a couple that were on and off for nearly the entire length of their relationship. After their first joint couples session, Diane didn't want to continue the sessions because she insisted that Pete was the real problem, and she would make certain that he would attend each and every appointment.

Pete continued with just about 50% commitment. Diane was right; he did feel free to talk about what was going on with him in her absence. He poured it all out, including his other girlfriend he had been seeing now for several months. In fact, he spilled his guts about his frustrations with how he was trying desperately to keep up appearances in both relationships.

When the subject of integrity came up, Pete was unfamiliar with the meaning. But once he understood that integrity and happiness are directly related, he knew he had to start telling the truth.

He left his new girlfriend and told Diane everything. After two weeks of being upset and "punishing" him, she let him back in. Three months later, he broke up with her.

The irony was not lost on Diane as she sat in my office. Seeing things from a more objective standpoint, she said, "I mean, how could I have expected him to respect me after I acted like a doormat?"

CHAPTER 20

Echoing the Past

"The people we are in relationship with are always a mirror, reflecting our own beliefs."
— Shakti Gawain, *Creative Visualization*

Many Love Addicts go through several Commitment Phobes until they change course. We feel as if we have somehow recreated the same guy over and over again. We often end up labeling all men as "bad" because it has been all we have known. We often do not realize that we are magnets, pulling these men toward us based on our own lack of self-worth.

Unwittingly, we continue to reel them in like fish because in between relationships, we don't stop to heal the cause. We just assume it was just one bad fish and take another dip in the lake. We blame the Commitment Phobe, perpetuating our victim status. *This one was different*, we thought. *This time we felt a real connection. This was finally it.* But didn't we say that about the last guy, too?

If there were men before the most recent Commitment Phobe, then we can see the underlying characteristics and similarities if we really look. If we had written and tracked all of the incidences, conversations, breakups, makeups and screwups, they would all likely fit the same basic profile.

SAME GUY, DIFFERENT FACE

If this was not your first serious relationship, the odds are grossly in your favor that the men who came before this guy carried many of the same commitment phobic qualities. But this last lap around the block felt more intense, more palpable and much more severe in emotion. As we persevere in our push/pull relationships, each new Commitment Phobe feels more intense than the last.

The *beginning* of the relationship with all of the past Commitment Phobes probably started much in the same way as the most recent. The more men we have experienced this pain with, the easier it is for us to line them all up in our minds and place the same sticker on them: Jerk. But did we really think that this most recent guy was the answer when we hadn't done anything in the meantime to fix the part of ourselves that was attracting them? We sure did! Suddenly, our sweet little lovebug was now shockingly in the same box as the others. *How could this have happened again*, we wondered.

LESSON LEARNED

After the last guy, we were sure this would never happen again. And when we met the current guy, we thought, "Thank God I finally found someone who is not an asshole." Ah, the memories.

In retrospect, we sought a guy who was the polar opposite of the last one, and yet nothing had changed internally to fix that broken magnet. No real emotional introspection or therapeutic venture had occurred. And if it had, we clearly got back on the horse too soon. Did we really expect a different result when we were still giving out the same vibration? It would be absolutely insane to think we could draw something new using the same old crayons and coloring book we've been using since we were kids. We will cover that childhood nightmare that led to therapy in a later chapter.

WOMEN'S INTUITION

For centuries, denying our intuition has been the source of many catastrophic events that could have been prevented had we only checked in with our gut. Although we think this may be the obvious thing to do, very few of us actually trust what we are feeling, mostly because we would rather stay in denial.

Our intuition is connected to who we are at our very core.

It is God, the Universe, Pure Love, Source Energy or whatever name we give our Higher Selves. But it is our biggest compass and our eternal cheer-leader. When something is nagging at our gut, we write it off as paranoia, lack of trust or rollover issues from our past relationships. Unless a real doctor with a real medical license has diagnosed us, our intuition is our best guide and should never be dismissed as crazy.

LIKE ATTRACTS LIKE

The Commitment Phobe and the Love Addict are attracted to each other immediately for good reason. They are both looking to be loved. The Commitment Phobe initiates a relationship with the Love Addict because he believes that she will never turn to face him. This is because in the *beginning* she may have appeared elusive and quite disinterested. On some level, she was attracted to him because he was relentless in his pursuit. When the Love Addict finally gave in to the chase, she never once thought that after much affection and attention that he would ever turn his back on her, having spent so much time on her tail.

Neither party really wants out of this otherwise tumultuous relationship. They are both gaining a great deal from this interaction. They are reliving old childhood personas and are simply perpetuating what they have always been accustomed to. Both the Love Addict and the Commitment Phobe are drawn to each other by a magnetic force. This is why the connection feels powerful and otherworldly. But we will undoubtedly attract a man who loves us equal in measure to how much we love ourselves.

If we think that we are not in control of attracting the Commitment Phobe to us, we may as well hang up our hats and retire from relationships for good. The truth is that we are in control of all of it. Yes, all of it. When we are not, we are simply letting someone else take the credit for our happiness, sadness and even hard-earned success. These perceptions keep us in victim mode.

Taking responsibility for the type of men we keep creating over and over again is critical to our recovery from love addiction.

Our prior issues with abandonment subconsciously cause us to recreate this scenario time and again. We could also be attracting the equivalent of what we think of ourselves in our most critical moments. Until we transform our inner lives and choose to live in a victimless state of mind, we will continually attract our good old friend, the Commitment Phobe.

BLURRED LINES

Similar to the Commitment Phobe, the Love Addict has a hard time differentiating between boundaries and walls. She tends to either spill her guts, drowning the Commitment Phobe in the process, or put up a wall (sharing nothing) to keep herself safe from pain. Both are unhealthy, and neither works as a means of protection. Healthy boundaries mean that the individual lets in the emotions of others to the point she is capable of handling. She also expresses her emotions in ways that are not harmful to her or others.

At certain points, the Love Addict may only use her

wall when dealing with the Commitment Phobe. This is usually her way of exerting strength, feeling that she is in the position of power and never letting her guard down again. Walls are dangerous and keep us from dealing with our problems, also causing a disconnect with those around us. Healthy boundaries keep us safe from harmful words and actions of others and allow us to be responsible for only our own feelings.

OWNING OUR REALITY

Taking responsibility is the most important thing we can do to be happy. When we know we are in charge of our failed relationships, we automatically gain power in creating better ones. We cannot move forward without questioning the past. Introspection and objectivity can become our most treasured assets if we are just willing to do the work. Besides, the only way we can change our relationships is by changing *ourselves*.

We will continue to attract only small amounts of love and affection until we have transformed our thoughts on who we are and what we ultimately deserve. Our relationships and our reactions to them are our responsibility. We are incapable of changing the Commitment Phobe, but we are perfectly capable of changing ourselves and who we attract to us.

NINA'S STORY

Length of Relationship: *Between nine months and two years.*

Commitment Phobic Attributes: *All of them.*

Nina was a typical Love Addict, caring deeply for her emotionally unavailable boyfriend at the expense of losing her pride and dignity. Her past relationships were very similar, and they all lasted approximately between nine months and two years. Each guy had a different job and personality, and each was unconscious that they were terrified of commitment and sought perfection. Nina spent countless days and nights wondering where she stood with these guys and getting the wool pulled over her eyes on several occasions.

When Nina was healed of her past push/pull relationships and began to create true love, she met Vince through a mutual friend. After a few dates, she came into my office for her weekly session, explaining that she had to end things with him. When I asked her why, she quickly retorted, "He used to be married!" She said she did not want a man who would leave a relationship or give up on marriage. It was probably my fault that I didn't explain to Nina earlier in her transition that getting married is a good sign and likely showed commitment. Unless, of course, he was a Married Commitment Phobe.

Finally, Nina's radar was clear, and her magnet was no longer able to attract the Commitment Phobe because she was already deep in the throes of self-love.

CHAPTER 21

The Power of Self-Love

"In the absence of love, we began slowly but surely to fall apart."
    - Marianne Williamson, *A Return to Love*

The Commitment Phobe did not bump into the Love Addict by accident. He was unable to give love, and she was unable to receive love. This subconscious dance draws them in with a magnetic force and makes for a difficult relationship. They are each looking for something that the other cannot offer. Both parties are searching for the missing piece that would complete the puzzle. Neither of them realizes that they are perpetuating old wounds and attracting to each other what they both lack: self-love. The Love Addict could never receive love from the Commitment Phobe. And the Commitment Phobe could never receive the love he looked for in the Love Addict. Because they both lack in the self-love department, they are unable to give away what they don't have. Sometimes, the Love Addict will pour all of her love into the Commitment Phobe, leaving her with nothing for herself.

The Love Addict is used to looking for love in places where she will never find it because the *last* place she looks is within. The most important relationship we can nurture is the one with ourselves. Our joy and self-worth lay at the very core of who we are. There is a reason that the Love Addict invites the Commitment Phobe into her reality. A woman with a healthy internal life and very few self-esteem issues regarding rejection, abandonment, abuse or loss will not readily attract this mysterious man into her life.

We accept the love we think we deserve at the *time* the Commitment Phobe appears. We can only attract love that is exactly comparable to the love we have for *ourselves*. The Love Addict is the ultimate hypocrite, looking for a man to love her while unable to fully love herself and give *herself* what she deserves.

When we learn to love and accept ourselves completely and unconditionally, our real Prince Charming will sweep us off our feet, and the Commitment Phobe will become a distant memory. I will cover that in a later chapter.

THE ORIGIN OF TRAUMA

The painful relationship with a Commitment Phobe can often force the Love Addict to confront her demons and seek out answers to this push/pull drama. There is an internal scream that may have been quieted and pushed out of earshot for many years. But we need to give that scream a voice to pull ourselves out of our dysfunctional relationship turmoil.

Childhood trauma can lead to adult drama in that we carry the weight of our past every day without even knowing it. The issues we suffered as children often stay with us on an unconscious level. The injustices that fell upon us long ago left an indelible mark on our self-esteem, self-worth and the physical, mental and emotional images we have of ourselves.

We may begin to recognize that we are living out our past selves in a way that is destructive to our well-being. We have to make a choice to begin again and create a new way of thinking and being. The problem is that knowing is only half the battle. Once we have the knowledge of why our behaviors and feelings are not in conjunction with reality, we can then start down the path toward the other fifty percent and begin to heal. To escape a painful past, we have to look it square in the eye, challenging it daily.

OUR INNER CRITIC

After our individual traumas, many of us spend our lives reiterating what was told or done to us as children. We took over where the abuse left off and unknowingly began our own destructive self-abuse and emotional annihilation. When the trauma occurred, whether emotional, verbal, physical, sexual or mental, we told ourselves that we deserved it and that, somehow, it was part of who we were. As a child, we weren't thinking logically, and eventually, we started to think that such ways of being in the world were normal. Some Love Addicts are attracted to a more emotionally unhealthy lifestyle because it can feel the most comfortable.

RELEASING THE VICTIM

No matter where or how we grew up, our backgrounds, races or cultures, we have all experienced trauma, abuse, rejection, brainwashing, teasing or belittling in some form. No one gets off scot-free where the human condition is concerned. But as adults, we know better, and we can choose our lives over again.

There is no need to be the victim in our own lives. Whether we are religious or not, we have still been given the freedom of choice, and along with our Higher Power, we are the creators of our destinies. Knowing that we are the choice makers, we then have complete control over where we go from here and who we want to be.

First, we don't have to be defined according to what was done to us. It's what we choose to do about it from this point forward that matters. We can retrain our minds to behave and function differently once we see our lives from an objective standpoint. We can stop victimizing ourselves at any moment, but we must choose to be uncomfortable at first to create a better life.

We can make choices that have nothing to do with our pasts.

We can create a new space for new beginnings. And we can do all of this by diligently facing our pain, our childhoods, our old thought patterns and our enemies (if only in our minds). All the while, we should remember that it isn't our past that holds us hostage; it's the dark thoughts that dwell within.

FORGIVENESS

To start the healing process and bury our childhood past for good, we must learn how to truly forgive. This includes forgiving our parents, our abusers and even our sexual assailants. This may seem like a massive undertaking at first, but it is necessary. Forgiveness does not mean what they did was acceptable. Forgiveness frees us to move on. It is helpful to view our abusers as broken themselves. After all, they also must have suffered their own traumas early in life. When we find compassion for the Commitment Phobe, forgiveness will naturally follow.

The most important person we need to forgive is ourselves. We spent many years behind an enclosed wall, hoping no one would discover how deeply wounded we really were. We had no control over what may have happened to us as children or as young adults. We do have control over healing the past, making new choices and moving forward.

ACCEPTING OURSELVES

The Love Addict is not broken, and there is nothing that she needs to fix to be worthy of love. Accepting the way we are, faults and all, gives us power and lets us off the hook instead of spending years trying to undo the past and our conditioning.

The incidences we may have suffered through as children will never fully leave us. They are a part of who we are. This may sound like miserable news, but it's just the way it works. (Lobotomies aren't a common practice anymore.) After we have undergone the forgiveness and healing processes, there will still be triggers that will unexpectedly throw us into an emotional tailspin. As long as we shine a bright light on our pain, it will have no power over us. Keeping it hidden in the dark causes it to grow, making it appear stronger and scarier. Ignoring our pain can lead to depression, anxiety, disease, unhappiness and deadly addictions.

We subconsciously react based on our past conditioning.

Moving forward, we can deal with "episodes" of

pain that can be triggered by the slightest thing by recognizing where they came from. We are then able to take personal responsibility for our actions and reactions to life and those around us. Our past has set us up for how we relate to life, but it needn't be that way when we choose to perceive differently.

My husband came home from work one day, and I asked him where the pizza was that I asked him to pick up for me due to my large workload. Feeling bad, he sheepishly told me that he forgot. Almost immediately, I started to cry. This was as much a surprise to me as it was to my poor husband. There I was crying over a pizza when I hadn't even cried over the recent passing of my dog! But when I questioned myself as to what was happening to me, I remembered an experience of being forgotten by my mother (this was the story I told myself as a child), which then caused an even stronger emotional reaction. My mother hadn't done anything wrong on purpose, but as a child, I told myself a different story and held tightly to my inner critic who liked to tell me how unimportant I was. This is just a small example of how our conditioning can cause adult episodes. But if we consistently check in with ourselves and diligently question every sentence, feeling, thought, action and reaction, we will eventually separate the past from the present and free ourselves from the binds of conditioning.

CREATING YOU

Once we have worked on our inner critic, compassion, forgiveness, acceptance and boundaries, we can choose to fill that old space with a new concept of ourselves.

After recognizing that we have the power to create our own lives in every new moment, our job is to take advantage of that empty void in our heart and fill it with who we want to become. Unless we transform our thoughts about who we are and what we want, nothing will ever change. We will just keep recreating the same scenarios, the same outcomes and the same Commitment Phobes. We have to rethink and challenge our old selves, releasing the victim and transforming into the creator. This may seem like a difficult task, but with a little faith, we can be exactly who we want to be and have everything we want in this life, including a healthy relationship with a committable man.

We often think that if only we had *that* creativity

or *that* grace or the positive attitude that woman exudes *then* we would be happier. Well, take it. It's yours! Decide who you want to become and practice your newfound way of being in the world. Perhaps you want to be more confident and outgoing. What does that look like? How does that manifest? How does that feel?

Choose what you do or don't want to possess.. Decide who you want to be and then *fake it until you make it*. You are a microcosm of the world you see around you. As Deepak Chopra says in *The Book of Secrets: Unlocking the Hidden Dimensions of Your Life*, "Never forget that you are not in the world; the world is in you."

INGRID'S STORY

Length of Relationship: *Ten months.*

Commitment Phobic Attributes: *Workaholic, self-absorbed, shutdown.*

Ingrid was madly in love with Cory, and after just a few months, they moved in together. He began to change after he was transferred to a new department at work, and his hours became grueling. When he wasn't working, he spent most nights drinking at the local pub with the guys and coming home late, if at all. He avoided Ingrid and refused to communicate what he was feeling about her and the relationship.

When Cory left Ingrid by means of a text message, she was devastated and mortified. Never in a million years did Ingrid imagine Cory could stoop so low. She thought for sure he was different. Over the next several months, she tried to shake herself out of shock while staring at her phone.

Convinced it wasn't over yet, Ingrid refused to do the work to find out how and why she created Cory in her life and what she could do to assure a Cory-free future. Spending months waiting for him to change his mind and realize the huge mistake he had made, Ingrid fell deeper into depression, losing work, weight, social outings and much-needed sleep.

Eventually, Ingrid realized that she didn't want a man who was afraid to commit and addicted to lying and avoiding her. She decided to get her act together and get busy creating a life filled with hope and oodles of self-love. After all, Ingrid thought, if she had held herself to a higher standard with Cory, would she have ever tolerated this imbalance in a relationship? No way.

Ingrid decided to spend the next several months in her own Relationship Rehab. She wrote letters in her journal to Cory, her parents and even her childhood abusers. She worked hard on forgiving them and, mostly, forgiving herself. She attended twelve-step meetings on codependency, read books on healing, listened to CDs from renowned spiritual teachers like Shakti Gawain, Debbie Ford, Marianne Williamson and Eckhart Tolle. Ingrid educated herself on the Law of Attraction and why she kept creating loss in her life. She learned that she didn't have to be the woman she was in the past, and that she could be whoever she wanted to be!

Ingrid rebuilt herself from the ground up. She developed grace, integrity, optimism, confidence and determination. For her secondary characteristics, she became nurturing, empathetic and fun. She wanted to be an early riser instead of a night owl.

She wanted to shed her wallflower persona and become more social. She wanted to take an art class and hone her creative side. She even quit her sales job and began working in her chosen field of advertising. During this exciting time of transformation, Ingrid knew she would still remain the same in many ways. She wanted to be the best Ingrid she could be, and that meant shedding her old baggage and packing a shiny new suitcase filled with her most desirable traits.

Today, Ingrid is married to a committed man, and they have a very healthy life together—the one they share and the one that is independent from the other. With grace and confidence, Ingrid now knows that she could not have been open to receiving unconditional love if she had never had unconditional love for herself.

CHAPTER 22

The Independent Woman

"We cultivate love when we allow our most vulnerable and powerful selves to be deeply seen and known."

- Brené Brown, *The Gifts of Imperfection*

During the relationship with a Commitment Phobe, the Love Addict replaces "me" with "we" and eventually puts herself on the back burner of her own life. If we have recognized the Love Addict within us throughout this book, then we are likely just scratching the surface of making some serious changes in our inner life. Among these is learning more independence, like not needing a man to feel worthy, lovable and unconditionally happy.

The Commitment Phobe is not attracted to the Independent Woman for the long-term. He can only magnetically attract women who are more love-addicted (codependent). This may come as a surprise given the idea that our independence may have been what drew him to us.

The Law of Attraction states that we attract what we feel we deserve. Therefore, our independent, happy-go-lucky persona we had in the *beginning* was almost like nature's mating call for the Commitment Phobe. Both parties subconsciously knew one was there to love and the other to leave. However, in the *beginning*, the Commitment Phobe is consciously drawn to the Love Addict because he thinks she is independent and will never enmesh him or request that they be intimate. The Love Addict may even have had her wall up in the *beginning*, making it appear as if she were uninterested in emotional intimacy.

Often times, we mistake independence with being cool, uncaring and closed off to our emotions. On the contrary, independence requires that we are *vulnerable* enough to open up to love. Many Love Addicts think the way they are portraying themselves to the external world is as follows: *I am independent because I do everything for myself. I don't need anyone, especially a man. I want the whole world to see that I am anything but needy.* The truth is that we *do* need others and we *do* need love and connection. We may not need a man, but we certainly need *people*.

Taking care of ourselves financially, emotionally and mentally is great, but closing ourselves off from love, outside help, advice and genuine connection does not make the perfect Independent Woman. No woman is an island, and pretending to be "too cool for school" can come at a high price. Our purpose on this planet is related to our ability to connect and feel love for others and ourselves.

CAREER AND SOCIAL LIFE

Finding a life purpose or passion can sometimes be more difficult than finding a country without a Starbucks! If you have not discovered your purpose yet, look at what gives you the most joy and start there. Money comes and money goes, but as long as it's always your own money coming and going, independence will remain in your hands.

The Independent Woman has friends outside of her love life and enjoys her time with them, focusing on things outside of her intimate relationship. Whether introverted or extroverted, the Independent Woman is defined by her self-love, her healthy boundaries, her trust in her inner guidance, her ability to give without losing herself and her acceptance of her flaws and faults.

INTEGRITY

When we have integrity, we will create a life filled with great expectations and even grander outcomes. When our actions directly back up our words, and we are consistent with our values, principles and ethics, we have integrity. The Love Addict leans more toward hypocrisy and away from integrity because she is focused on survival and getting the love she craves from others. She is unable to back up her words with actions because half of the time, she isn't even paying attention to anything other than getting what she needs.

Long periods of happiness and peace of mind are marks of integrity. When the Independent Woman lives a life filled with honesty and truth, she can't help but feel good. When we have integrity, we take personal responsibility, and the universe backs us up. Taking responsibility for attracting the Commitment Phobe into our lives helps us change our internal world. The Independent Woman attracts the love she deserves.

BALANCE

Maintaining a balance of family life, social life,

work life and personal life can be challenging. But this balance is necessary for our inner life to thrive. The Independent Woman can do it all, even if she wants to scream at times! In contrast, it is difficult for the Love Addict to focus on other areas of her life with presence and clarity.

When she is currently in a relationship with the Commitment Phobe, her life is off-balance because of her love addiction. It is completely possible and healthy to be independent and still have a committed relationship with a man as long as we have boundaries and keep ourselves as our number one priority.

VULNERABILITY

For the Love Addict to maintain her persona of businesswoman, perfect girlfriend, happy wife or independent single gal, she sometimes ignores her softer side, her true feminine nature. This important side of herself needs to be shown to the world and to the men in her life. To create true connection and happiness, there is only one way: the Independent Woman must pay diligent and personal attention to the vulnerability factor.

The Love Addict can often be confused about

what emotions are appropriate to convey and what could possibly scare away prospective suitors. This confusion is largely due to a lack of self-worth and unhealthy boundaries. It's important to recognize that vulnerability takes courage. Behind a wall of seemingly astute strength, the Love Addict feels she can protect herself from abandonment. In addition, she has to be willing to take the risk of opening up, letting others in and being completely truthful about her feelings, issues, sadness, insecurities and needs. Not an easy feat.

It's actually fairly easy to appear strong and without needs.

We are quite used to the idea of putting on a brave face to move through life. Women are told men aren't attracted to weak women, so we believe we should never open up, confusing weakness with vulnerability. In actuality, vulnerability requires great strength.

Being independent does not mean being alone and walling off the outside world or the people in it. Quite the contrary, it means loving yourself so much that you are free to be exactly who you are at all times. It means you are free from needing love from men to survive. It means not seeking approval from your peers and being open and vulnerable. The Independent Woman is not afraid to appropriately express her feelings and insecurities, for she understands that perfection is an illusion. She embraces her fears and phobias, knowing they are a normal part of the human experience.

In the throes of vulnerability, interdependence will then take form, and a connection with a committable man can feel amazing. Due to healthy boundaries, the Independent Woman can be autonomous after engaging in intimacy with her partner. Being vulnerable requires trust.

If your perfectly normal insecurities and flaws scare away a prospective suitor, then there is a high probability that suitor is a Commitment Phobe. A committable man will not be scared away by your "needing" him. He is happy to be your knight in shining armor, rescuing you from your pain. The committable man loves you for all that you are, feeling good about himself and your connection.

HAPPILY SINGLE

We have all heard the stories about finding love

when it's least expected, and the truth is that when we aren't looking for love, we are much more content. We aren't dealing with dating sites, blind dates, and the casual bar chat or annual company party with one eye on every single guy who enters the room. The Independent Woman knows that the Law of Attraction works, and she will energetically pull in the committable man based solely on the love she feels for herself. She knows what she wants and deserves, magnetically attracting a like-minded man.

When the Independent Woman goes out for dinner with her friends, her smile says it all, and she emanates self-assurance. She is not desperate for a man, nor is she concerned about attracting one. When she thinks about a future relationship, she is excited but not hurried. She is happy *with* one, but also happy *without* one. With faith and trust in the universe, her inner feelings of confidence and love will bring her the perfect man at the perfect time.

SEX AND DATING

Many of us may need to relearn how to date. Often, we feel the pressure of sticking with the conventional rules and guidelines, specifically regarding sex. But that was our old life; the Independent Woman thinks for herself and trusts her own unique instincts.

No matter what age, culture or religion, women everywhere deal with the issue of sex. When it comes to the rules of dating and when to engage in the physical act of love, we tend to either over-analyze or undermine its value and purpose. The Love Addict may confuse sex with love, getting hurt in the process.

It's the 21st century, and sex is not what it was for our grandparents. However, as women, we don't need to be subjected to the rules of society or how magazines say we should behave. We must learn to listen to our own emotional guidance and physical bodies. Not all women are the same, and not all rules fit everyone. By being our own healthy decision-makers, we can take back control over our individual minds without being governed by outside influences or by what we were told when we were young.

For example, when it comes to sex, many women have a four-to-seven-date rule. But placing rules on our dating lives is like planning for the apocalypse. No one knows exactly what it will look like or feel like on any given day. It's much more fun to let ourselves live in the unknown with no expectation, allowing for the unexpected.

Regulating when we will engage in intimacy should never be overly planned, or it loses its primary functions of connection and fun. Know your own limitations and follow your own inner guidance. When it comes to the decision to have sex in a new relationship, it's important that we are not filling an emotional void. Knowing who we are, knowing what we want and being responsible for our self-worth is vital. Sex is no substitute for self-love.

AMY'S STORY

Length of Relationship: *Eight months.*

Commitment Phobic Attributes: *Fear, insecurity, indecision.*

Amy was convinced that she had to be strong to keep her "boyfriend" Patrick from pulling away. And she wasn't all wrong. As a Commitment Phobe, Patrick shuddered at the first sign of enmeshment and never committed to calling Amy his girlfriend. So, to keep him on his toes and wanting more, she denied him love and affection. She would only wait for him to call her, never initiating contact because she did not want to appear needy. This originally worked, causing Patrick to panic and run toward Amy because he needed to be loved, too.

Once Amy realized that calling Patrick would make him run for the hills, she refused to let him think she needed him at all. Within this push/pull relationship, Patrick had a bad habit of coming and going, hemming and hawing and generally being indecisive. Amy became the Lady-in-Waiting, expecting the tides to turn in her favor.

Due to Patrick pulling away whenever she would open up, Amy refused to show her true self, share her feelings or even look to him for advice. Patrick was losing out on the opportunity to make Amy happy. Amy's idea of putting up a façade with false feelings was only a prelude to prolonging the inevitable end of this courtship. Due to her wall always being up, the connection eventually faded. Patrick broke up with Amy because he felt it was a "one-sided" relationship, even though he was also guilty of sabotaging the intimacy.

While mourning the loss of Patrick and allowing herself to understand her abandonment fears,

Amy began to find balance. She planned weekends with her friends (instead of saving them for Patrick), joined a yoga class, changed jobs and started working toward her passion as a musician. Her life changed when she put the cart before the horse by beginning to live the life she had imagined. For the first time in years, Amy was truly happy and thriving. She found her independence when she found her self-acceptance. Amy learned it was okay to need somebody as long as it wasn't out of desperation or seeking love to replace loneliness.

Not surprisingly, several months into her newfound bliss, Patrick called and confessed he had made a mistake and wanted another chance. Amy was simply uninterested in going back to a stressful relationship that revolved around her need to play games.

CHAPTER 23

Introducing the Committed Man

"The most creative act you will ever undertake is the act of creating yourself."
- Deepak Chopra, *The Way of the Wizard*

After years, or even decades, of pushing, pulling and prodding, it's finally time to release the confusion, pain, frustration and depression, and put the Commitment Phobe to rest. As soon as we embrace this new way of thinking, we will serendipitously reign in our knight in shining armor who we have been looking for all along.

Now that we are self-loving, deserving, and independent and have a clear understanding of who we are, the Committed Man can enter the picture. Once we have transformed from a Love Addict into a healthy Independent Woman, we will instantly know when we have snagged this rare gem.

This amazing new guy is committed, affectionate, open, loving, caring, honest, respectful and loyal. And the best part is that he doesn't get scared away when he gets too close! In fact, he enjoys his closeness with you and embraces intimacy. You are saving money on psychics and seminars because there is no longer a need to question where he goes and what he does.

Luckily, you don't need a can opener to get into his mind.

Does this man actually exist? Of course! You were just never going to meet him with your outdated concept of yourself. We attract to us what we believe we deserve (even subconsciously), and up until now, that wasn't much. Because when we know better, we create better.

THE COMMITTED MAN

A Committed Man feels good when his partner is happy. The happier his girlfriend or wife, the more he feels he is doing his job. He isn't scared of his feelings or what lies underneath.

Unlike the Commitment Phobe, the Committed Man has a healthy thought process when it comes to intimacy, fear and decision-making. His outer confidence is genuine, and he doesn't feel the need to overcompensate due to hidden insecurities or lie about who he really is. He does not exaggerate the truth in an attempt to make himself look better in the eyes of his lovers and peers. His ego is intact, and he doesn't care much about outside opinions when it comes to love. The Committed Man has a balanced life, dispelling any mystery. He is confident in himself and trusts his own decisions, including his choice in a life partner. He has no desire to keep searching for another woman because he has you.

DECISIVELY CONFIDENT

A Committed Man knows what he wants and is capable of making decisions regarding his life, home, family, career, finances and relationships. He does not sway in whatever direction the wind takes him. He is in control of his inner and outer world.

Perhaps the most distinguishing characteristic is that the Committed Man is confident in a normal, healthy way. He doesn't come across as the Charmer because he is not looking to charm his way into your pants. He knows that to get the girl, he only needs to rely on being himself. He has no need to manipulate you into liking him because he feels quite comfortable with who he is.

The Committed Man may not have a million bells and whistles to counter the Commitment Phobe's desperate charm and witty ways, but this is exactly what got us in trouble in the first place. This is not to say that a Committed Man is boring! It is just that he does not come with all the mysterious guesswork that the Commitment Phobe does, giving the new relationship a different feeling, one of inner peace and deep trust.

FEARLESS INTIMACY

A Committed Man does not see his partner as needy but rather as someone secure enough to express her insecurities, desires and needs. Rather than feeling suffocated, a Committed Man feels good when his partner needs him.

The Commitment Phobe pursued the Love Addict because he was hoping she would never enmesh him, suffocate him or insist on any type of real intimacy. (What was he thinking?) After all, the Love Addict was elusive, playful and unapproachable in the pre-beginning. Luckily, the Committed Man is not interested in playing these games. He is looking for a woman who is open and available. He wants to give and receive love equally.

It is not of any interest to the Committed Man to stop having physical intimacy because what healthy, normal man does not want to have sex? He does not lose his sexual desire for his partner after the first year or two. In fact, his sex drive is perfectly healthy, and he enjoys the connection much like you do. The Committed Man is not afraid of love, intimacy and closeness, and he doesn't attract women who are.

A COMMITTED PAST

If he is over a reasonable age, the Committed Man has had one or more long-term relationships, likely lasting over two years without any "breaks" during the courtship. Now, he may think some of his exes were a little crazy, but he does not feel the need to delegate blame on anyone. The Committed Man knows his faults and where he went wrong, causing him to want to do better the next go-round. He takes responsibility for his past without passing too much judgment in any direction.

Amongst the many differences between the Committed Man and the Commitment Phobe is how he leaves his relationships. Unlike his counterpart, when a Committed Man is no longer interested in being in a relationship, he commits to leaving and doesn't keep changing his mind.

Remember, this is a guy who is comfortable with his decisions and has a healthy connection to his own feelings and instincts. He doesn't cause a big fight to get away or leave with no warning due to some fictitious undiagnosed mood disorder. When a Committed Man falls out of love or decides the connection is not great, he will actually relay this information, face to face.

THE SOUL MATE MYTH

Many philosophers, relationship experts, spiritual teachers and gurus believe that we each have a couple thousand soul mates in the world. That's not a lot considering that there are more than seven billion people on the planet. It would be likened to the number of people at Disneyland on a Tuesday afternoon compared to the entire planet Earth. But this is really good news. Isn't it nice to know there are a few thousand men that will tolerate our faults, insecurities, temperaments, PMS and general female mood swings? Shocking when you really think about it!

Alongside the unwritten law that the Universe is

always looking out for our best possible outcome, the odds that we have already bumped into a few of our soul mates in life thus far are pretty high. The Commitment Phobe could very well have been one of them. This does not mean that you are meant to be together.

A HEALTHY RELATIONSHIP

After we have finally said goodbye to our love addicted past, we are ready to be in a healthy relationship. The push/pull relationship is far from healthy, and many of us may not even know what healthy looks like anymore. Let's just say that it doesn't look like begging, weeping, confusion and desperation in the form of ebbing passion and lust. The Committed Man is not afraid to commit, but having a healthy relationship with *this* guy requires different ingredients and a new way of embracing interdependence. A healthy relationship means appreciating, trusting and accepting the Committed Man, things foreign to the Love Addict's vocabulary.

COLLEEN'S STORY

Length of Relationship: *Six years.*

Commitment Phobic Attributes: *None.*

Colleen was a classic Love Addict. She was manipulative, analytical, calculating, worrisome, codependent and felt undeserving of love. At age 30, she had already spent the better part of her adult life chasing after men who would abandon her. With her worst breakup occurring after a bad marriage, Colleen decided it was time for a change. She spent her days in therapy, healing spiritually from her repeated losses. She meditated at night, asking for guidance and peace of mind.

Having healed herself, Colleen was alone and happy for the first time in her life. Soon after, Colleen began to casually date, never wondering *if this was The One* after each date. She simply enjoyed her time with men without any attachment or expectation. After all, she didn't need it. She had herself now.

When Colleen met Jeff, a Committed Man, it wasn't exactly love at first sight. She knew she felt great around him but was unsure how to move forward into a commitment, having only been five months out of a relationship with a Commitment Phobe. Jeff pursued her from an appropriate distance, and Colleen felt an unexplainable pull toward him. She finally gave in, and they be-

Introducing the Committed Man

gan to date. They fell in love rather quickly and married a year later. They have two children and are continuing to grow as a family. Both are consciously committed and happily married.

CHAPTER 24

Creating a Committed Man

"If I am committed to myself and to living my truth, I will attract others with equal commitment."

- Shakti Gawain, *Living in the Light*

To sit back, relax and leave the door open for our Prince Charming, we must first be very specific about exactly who we want to walk through that door. By not specifying exactly who we want to the universe, we open ourselves up to anyone. This can be a ton of fun for serial daters, but if we are ready for The One, we have to home in on what we want. If we leave ourselves open to meeting someone and anyone, we will eventually get them quite easily. There are many *someones* and *anyones*. In fact, they are *everywhere*. This can be very time-consuming, not to mention frustrating.

The good news is that the Law of Attraction states that to get exactly what we want, we must first experience exactly what we don't want. We can certainly thank the Commitment Phobe for that. Recognizing that he was quite instrumental in helping us realize what we don't want in a man helps us find gratitude for our past failed relationships. We should never regret our past, the men we have dated or the time we spent with them. Everything and everyone from our past has brought us precisely to where we need to be in this very moment.

But if we really knew that the power to create true love lies in our own hands, we would certainly be using this very special tool, wouldn't we? We put so much effort into finding the perfect job, the perfect home and even the perfect pair of jeans. All the while, we are wondering why we cannot find the perfect man. After all, who are we really buying those jeans for anyway?

In our search for the Committed Man, we often wonder why our friend, Fate, keeps letting us down. It can be very easy to lose faith in Fate. But the real power comes in knowing that we have a huge hand in creating our own lives. We have to trust in her and allow her in after we have been clear about self-love, self-acceptance and whom we are asking her for.

THE LIST

If I had a nickel for every time I heard, "I just want a nice guy, is that too much to ask?" I could purchase a parking lot in New York's Times Square. The real problem is not that this is too much to ask. The real problem is that it is not enough to ask. I have known many "nice" alcoholics, "nice" non-committal men, "nice" guys with no passion, "nice" guys with no sense of humor and "nice" guys that still live with their parents. The question is, do you want more than just nice? Many well-intentioned women end up with the wrong men simply because they are not being specific enough.

The problem is that we think a nice guy is easier to obtain than a guy with a longer list of characteristics. We think the odds are with us because there are a million nice guys out there. We feel that if we are too specific in our desires, we will never get what we want because it would be like finding a needle in a haystack. The truth is that if we want true love and happiness with a Committed Man, we must be specific. Settling for whatever comes our random little way is not an option.

Making a master list of all the attributes you seek in your dream guy and knowing without a doubt that he's coming is the best thing you can do to prepare his path to you. Write down at least 90 attributes, traits and desires. The more specific, the faster he will arrive. Do you want a man who is compassionate, affectionate, loyal, honest, enjoys traveling, cooks, seeks adventure, has many friends and paints in his free time? Or would you rather have a man that dons a suit to the office, kisses you before work every morning, wants five kids and fights for animal rights? It's all up to you! But remember, fate will do nothing but bring you what you feel you deserve and what you feel is possible.

THE VISION BOARD

I know, I know. The old vision board assignment. But creating a visual really can help to manifest the Committed Man!

A vision board is a large canvas, poster board or drawing paper with magazine cutouts or pictures of people, words, places, desires, images and thoughts on what you want your future together to look like or how you want your future to feel. The vision board can be a useful tool in creating the Committed Man. Sift through old magazines and look for words and pictures that match your list. Clip photos out of where you see the two of you, such as the beach, the Greek Isles or a beautiful home. You can add children, animals, nature, religious symbols or anything that makes you happy to look at.

JUST IMAGINE

In the bestselling novel, *Jonathan Livingston Seagull*, Richard Bach writes, "To fly as fast as thought, to anywhere that is, you must begin by knowing that you have already arrived." In other words, to have the future you want, you must start by living it today through the power of your imagination.

Along with making your specific list and vision board, it is important that you really *feel* the Committed Man as if he already exists. Lie in bed, close your eyes and feel the warmth of him near you. Imagine he is there. What does he smell like? What is he wearing? What does he feel like? How are you feeling lying next to him? Do you feel safe?

When we practice pretending that he is already here, that he exists before he enters our lives, the

Universe will match that desire. Begin by feeling the excitement and relief of finally having the man of your dreams. Revel in your hard work and smile, knowing that you created your loving Committed Man. Close your eyes and know he is with you until this imaginary life feels as real as the dirt under your feet.

THE JOURNAL

Putting our desires on paper can be a powerful tool in creating everyday magic. Buy a brand-new journal, one that makes you feel good to look at and touch. Write about the vacations you are taking with him. Write about how amazing he already is and how impressed your friends and family are by his love and adoration of you. Be sure to write in the present tense, making this real in the moment. As like attracts like, you will energetically have the feeling that matches your current state of being.

Perhaps imagine you recently returned from a long vacation with this amazing new man. Write about the walk on the beach you had with him, detail the plane ride, the beautiful sunset and how you felt. Perhaps he proposed to you, and you felt a sense of security and safety rush through your veins. Whatever imaginary scenarios you choose to write about, it is the feeling underneath the words that you want to uncover and hold onto.

THE "HOW"

For years now, single women have been looking for love through blind dates, online sites, local bars, churches, AA, meetups, greet-ups and the produce aisle. But there may be no need to look anywhere. The great thing about fate is after we have decided exactly who we are and who we want to create, we then look forward to his arrival with positive anticipation. How we will meet this man will happen on its own.

When it comes to searching for The One, it is the searching that will certainly get us nowhere fast. If we trust in the Universe, love ourselves unconditionally and leave the house every so often, we are destined to meet our mate. If we knew our horse was riding in with certainty, then it will happen. Let's just hope he doesn't *look* like a horse.

ALLOWING

It is vital to the creation process that we allow the Committed Man to enter. If we are so busy with lists, vision boards and journals all the time, we never make room for allowing him into our lives. It is in the allowing that everything takes material form. Most of us are so busy creating that we forget to stop and allow.

It is imperative that we remain happy and hopeful in the process of allowing the Committed Man in. Whenever possible, raise your vibration and energy and do whatever makes you *feel good*. This is more important than any other step. When we go about life feeling frustrated, depleted and discouraged that our Prince Charming has not yet arrived, we keep him from coming in simply because we attract what we feel.

CLARITY AND APPRECIATION

The Committed Man wants the Independent Woman to be direct, open and clear. He never received the Commitment Phobe's manual for girl-code: beating around the bush, dropping mysterious hints and passive-aggressively looking for affection.

Women want someone to listen, but when a man listens to our problems, he immediately wants to draw us an escape route out of the scary forest. Then we get annoyed because he may not have gotten the memo that we just wanted a friendly ear.

When he offers advice, sometimes it is good to pretend to take it, even if we don't. We can always discard it later. Think of it as a terrible sweater you got for Christmas but plan on returning. On the flip side, men don't want our friendly, unsolicited advice. This makes them feel like we don't trust in their decision-making abilities, something the Committed Man takes pride in.

Being clear, being kind and making requests of what we need can simplify things. Men aren't mind readers, and we can never assume they know what we want every minute of the day.

When we appreciate the little things, the little things appreciate. In other words, the Committed Man will unknowingly want to do more for us when he feels a greater amount of appreciation for the things he does. Whether it's mowing the lawn, making coffee, taking the kids out for a few hours or working overtime. Appreciate all of it, and let him know! Don't worry, the women's liberation movement is still intact. But there are innate characteristics of men and women that will never change. Our DNA carries variants of these given roles: the hero and the damsel.

When we trust the Committed Man to get things done in the world, he feels encouraged to do more and be more. When he comes home from the store and forgets our favorite cereal, make him feel that it's no big deal. When we suddenly start nagging him about how annoyed we are because we told him twice and wrote it down, we are sending his masculinity out the window.

LOVE AND ACCEPTANCE

Not sweating the small stuff is the best-kept secret in relationships. But with the Committed Man, this comes much more easily because it is all small stuff. Unlike the last one, your new relationship is full of love, *real* love. Not the kind that punishes, gets even, hopes someone loses or fights to be on top.

When we love our Committed Man, and we don't try to change him, he feels accepted. And in return, we get a much happier man. When we were with the Commitment Phobe, it felt like all we did was try to change him. In a healthy relationship, both parties are much less interested in teaching, controlling or directing one another to *fit* the mold.

MONICA'S STORY

Length of Relationship: *One year and six months.*

Commitment Phobic Attributes: *Indecisive, self-absorbed, verbally abusive, angry, shut down.*

Monica and Aaron were picture-perfect on the outside. He was a corporate manager in high demand, and she was a sales representative for a popular retail store. Behind closed doors, Aaron would call Monica a "crazy bitch" during arguments or when he was in a bad mood.

Always finding new ways to push her away, Aaron preferred to keep his feelings hidden and his affections at bay. But when she finally caught him cheating with an ex-girlfriend, she left him. Aaron cried and promised to change, but Monica had heard it all before and refused to fall for his manipulations again.

Monica was almost emotionally disabled with the thought that she would never find someone like her ex. And, even though Aaron was a Commitment Phobe, she still compared every guy to him, and no one ever added up. The problem was that she would rather have jumped from one guy to the next than take her chances of being alone and single. But lucky for Monica, as fate would have it, she didn't meet another Aaron. Instead, she gave up and decided to be single.

In the months following her breakup, Monica decided that she did not want to end up with another guy with commitment issues, and she was determined not to repeat her past. She instead spent her time committed to herself and her recovery from love addiction by meditating, keeping a journal, facing her past, accepting her "flaws" and learning to love herself unconditionally.

CHAPTER 25

Happiness as a Way of Life

"Success, wealth, good health and nurturing relationships are by-products of happiness, not the cause."

- Deepak Chopra, *The Ultimate Happiness Prescription*

To create true love, we must find our inner joy before love can find us. If we find that we are unhappy most of the day, we will invite in more of that feeling. This is how the Commitment Phobe slips through the cracks, showing up as a happy, charming, committable man who eventually turns. Our energy is only going to bring in what we put out authentically. Pretending to be happy will only bring in other pretenders, the Commitment Phobe included.

We can begin by understanding that while we do need connection with ourselves and others to be our happiest, we do not need a man to be happy.

Not even Tom Cruise could complete Katie Holmes. We are never incomplete. We must first be complete in our own inner happiness prior to having the blissful fairy tale ending. We should ideally have a feeling of unconditional love already, so that if no man ever came along, we would still be happy. This is the space in which we meet the Committed Man.

Let's be honest here, what we really want at the end of the day is to fall asleep with a smile, whether in a relationship or simply loving ourselves as our most valuable relationship. All efforts toward this goal can be attributed to almost every single thing we do, think and say throughout the day.

THE FUTURE

We seek happiness in the future. We think one day, when we are rich, find the right mate, have children or obtain security, we will finally be happy. We assume once all of our needs are met, we will be rewarded with peace of mind. But life never stops moving, and we never get to stop creating. We are works in progress, continually seeking ways to express who we really are. Instead, we search for that *one* day where we can take a deep breath and bask in knowing we have *finally* made it to our destination. But I have yet to meet any-one, young, old or on their deathbed, who has reached this fantasy island.

When we look to the past and the future, happiness appears to live within an illusory veil of time. But science clearly states that time and space do not exist. So where is true happiness, and how can we find it?

The Universe is magnificent. If we truly begin to comprehend the power of our own ability to create, we can master our lives. Nothing appears in our lives by coincidence. We have placed it all in front of ourselves with our thoughts and feelings, the good and the bad. The Universe always gives us more of what we focus on.

THE PRESENT

As Deepak Chopra points out in *The Path Made Clear*, now is the point of arrival. And there is nothing more blindingly true than this moment. It is where we create, build dreams and find our joy. There is no future yet, and there is nothing "out there" in the great beyond that holds the key to our happiness. Although our mind will tell us repeatedly that there is.

Everything that exists can only exist right now. The energy of happiness is everywhere around you, inside you, above you and below you. You are bathing and basking in it. But the moment we seek it outside ourselves in the future, we lose it.

We start focusing our attention away from the present and away from happiness. We only need to allow ourselves the happiness that is already ours in this moment. To obtain this state of joy, we virtually need to do *nothing*.

When we accept things exactly as they are, it's like choosing to live. Accepting people for who they are is one of the hardest things to do. Whether they are good, bad, pleasant, unpleasant, sad, quiet, gay or straight, we should *choose* them how they are, even the Commitment Phobe. Trying to change someone is one of the biggest mistakes we make. We would have better luck changing the color of the sky.

Byron Katie, author of *Loving What Is*, says, "As long as you think that the cause of your problem is 'out there'—as long as you think that anyone or anything is responsible for your suffering—the situation is hopeless. It means that you are forever in the role of victim, that you're suffering in paradise." Accepting life and the present moment as it is can be an empowering choice. We suddenly know that we are the creators of our destinies, and all things are perfectly in order. Happiness is the acceptance of life just as it is and just as it is not.

HEALTH

One study has shown that "health, not wealth, determines happiness." According to a study of the Economic Determinants of Happiness based on data gathered by the U.S. Census, "health is a far more powerful determinant of an individual's happiness than his or her income. Self-described 'healthy' people are 20 % happier than average, while 'unhealthy' people are 8.25% less happy." (Mims, 2012) There are many ways in which we can feel healthier and live happier lives, hence attracting a Committed Man at lightning speed.

Eating Right

The foods we put into our bodies correlate indirectly with our levels of happiness. Taking care of ourselves should be our number one priority, and to be truly self-sufficient and independent, we have to pay diligent attention to our health. Eating fresh organic fruits, vegetables and whole grains can affect our moods drastically. With good moods, we create good relationships!

Exercise

Burning calories is an easy way to raise our serotonin levels and look great at the same time. Doctors estimate that between 65% and 85% of the world's population do not exercise enough. And the American Psychological Association reports that exercise, in any form, helps reduce depression by burning cortisol.

Yoga can do wonders for the mind, body and spirit.

Scientific studies reveal that yogis score high on the happiness charts as Dr. R.M. Matthijs Cornelissen of the Sri Aurobindo Ashram in Pondicherry, India, explains, "In the Vedic tradition, *ananda*, or delight, is seen as being present in the essence of everything that exists. Happiness is thus not something that depends on what you have, but what you are." (Pirisi, 2017)

Nature and all its beauty is our gift from the Universe to enjoy free of charge whenever we choose. The smell of fresh air on a nighttime walk in the neighborhood can do wonders for our joy. According to research in the journal, Environmental Health and Technology, "exercising in natural areas is not only good for your physical health—it can improve your mood and sense of well-being in as little as five minutes. " (Graber, 2010)

Meditation

Sitting in silence and allowing the moment to take over is a powerful tool for finding our joy. Meditating for 30 minutes every morning can change our lives, and we don't even have to get out of bed! It reminds us that we have a space to go within whenever our day gets hectic. Stress, worry and fear can be nearly eliminated with consistent daily meditation.

Philanthropy

Giving to others opens our hearts and lets love breathe. Happiness can then circulate and free itself from being trapped. Giving can be as simple as listening to a friend or helping anyone without expecting something in return. Giving freely means both participants receive joy, making this one of the most efficient ways to reach happiness. Obviously, volunteering at a shelter, supporting the elderly, feeding the homeless and tithing to your local charity are all ways in which you can generate even more joy. And when we feel good, good things come our way, including Mr. Right, the Committed Man.

GRATITUDE AND PERCEPTION

Being appreciative of everything in our lives is a straight line toward happiness. Dwelling in what we wish we had, what we don't have and who has more than us is the foundation for misery, grief and even war. One of the worst things we can do is focus on what we don't have. Instead, we must focus on the things we do have to generate more.

We are happiest when we breathe in gratitude and give thanks for life's simplest pleasures. It is in the present that gratitude lives. When we feel gratitude, the Universe sends us more things to be grateful for. When we focus on negativity and lack, the Universe will give us more unwanted issues to complain about.

Changing our perception of who are, where we are, what we have and what we don't have is the most beneficial tool in our emotional toolbox. In this sense, happiness is only a perception away.

We can literally choose to see our lives and ourselves differently right now. As Wayne Dyer says, "Change the way you look at things, and the things you look at change." (Dyer, Success Secrets)

BE THE CHANGE

Until we take responsibility for the good and the bad that we have created in our lives, we have absolutely no control over our future. Our lives would feel like a runaway train headed into the abyss of anything, everything or nothing. We are the captains of our own ships, and even if God, the Source, the Universe, Jesus or Buddha is on our team, we still have the free will to create our path.

We wanted the right person, but seldom did we think about *being* the right person. We have many expectations for the Committed Man, but we must also meet these same expectations ourselves, bringing balance to create a healthy relationship.

GREAT EXPECTATIONS

When we have true happiness and unconditional love, we will find the man who loves us unconditionally. He will appear when we least expect it at the airport, the local flea market or on the street. When love and happiness are present, and when we are walking around with a smile, a Committed Man will come into the picture. It is no myth that we will find him when we are not looking. This happens because normally when we are searching for love, our quest is usually sparked by the fear of being alone and never finding that special someone. Hence, we are searching out of necessity, not out of the joy of expectancy.

When we focus on the love we have for ourselves, our family and our friends, love surrounds us and ignites a feeling of joy. This is the only feeling we need to find the Committed Man. Being authentic and willing to receive the love of another is key. Have a glass of wine, laugh with your friends and talk about the magic reality that is your life. Possibilities are endless, and we can create the exact relationship we want.

SUFFERING AND WORTH

Believe it or not, too many intelligent, educated adults believe that we are meant to suffer in our lives. They believe that it's only *after* we suffer enough and "pay our dues" that we can collect our reward.

We were not born to suffer, and we were certainly not born to be denied love. We came here to create, to love and to experience our innate joy in a whole new way. The reason we love being happy is that it is our natural state. If suffering were our *natural* state, we would enjoy *that*.

The problem is that many of us were brought up to believe that life is supposed to be hard and we need to fight for what we want. We believe there are good and bad, right and wrong, yes and no. We did not grow up to believe that we are to see the good in every situation. To see the opportunity in suffering and grow from pain is the route to happiness and the Committed Man.

We know better now. We know that we have a choice, and we can choose happiness at every turn. And when we feel sad, angry, frustrated or worried, we understand that happiness lies beneath those feelings, and it will find its way through.

Being worthy of love is our birthright. We don't need to be, do, act, have, imply or ascertain anything to have that innate worth. We just have to breathe. And even that is up for debate. The Love Addict is insistent that she really loves the Commitment Phobe and stays with him because of that one simple reason. But how can you love somebody who treats you like a second-class citizen? Who looks out for his own needs without being concerned about yours? The Love Addict has a skewed definition of love. Luckily, real love doesn't make you paranoid, jealous, miserable, suspicious or scared.

There is no need to fix or change who we are before meeting the Committed Man. But after we find that unconditional love for ourselves, the love that we were born with, we begin to notice that finding a man is not a priority.

THE PEANUT BUTTER CUP

Along with many others, I believe that we are here on this planet to experience who we are. And who we are is eternal love and joy.

I truly believe that we are pure loving energy, and before incarnating into flesh, we were unable to actually experience that. Hence, our human minds and bodies come in handy. We can now experience ourselves *experientially*.

Let me explain it this way. It's as if you were a peanut butter cup, and you knew you tasted great (because that's what all the chocolate experts are saying), but you couldn't taste yourself because you *are* the cup. Therefore, you (the peanut butter cup) create a human with a mouth and taste buds, so you can taste yourself.

You are the peanut butter cup, and you are the person eating the peanut butter cup. We are pure love, and we can now experience the pure love that we are. Problems arise when we forget that we are the peanut butter cup and start to believe we are the flesh that we created to taste it.

This little metaphor is what works for me; that doesn't make it relatable to everyone. It is simply true for me. We should always follow what makes us feel good, and that is individual to everyone. Buddha said, "Believe nothing, no matter where you read it or who has said it, no matter if I have said it, unless it agrees with your own reason and your own common sense." (Garfinkel, 2008)

Many people spend their entire lives searching for happiness. Some look for it in others, and others seek it in mind-altering substances. Many seek it in expensive homes, fancy cars, new clothing, furniture, social status, fame, money or personal appearances. They don't realize that these things are associated with the ego (which is fine), but the ego is not the part responsible for or able to find our happiness. The ego is the flesh we created to help the peanut butter cup. The peanut butter cup is the happiness.

YOUR STORY

Length of Relationship: *Forever.*

Commitment Phobic Attributes: *None.*

Out of all the fabulous women in the Universe, you are at the top of the pack with your introspection, gratitude and fearlessness. Take these attributes and make time to begin a new life with a new you. You are valuable beyond words simply because you exist. You are important. If you suddenly ceased to exist on the planet, the world would be a different place, and the cosmos would shake amidst your departure. It is critical that you understand your unique value, and it is time to allow yourself to love yourself *just as you are.* You *are* perfection.

With high intentions, an amazing man awaits you on your one-of-a-kind journey through life. He is committed, supportive, loving, generous, kind, sexy, loyal, caring, affectionate, charming, confident, open, determined, easy-going, warm, honest and genuine, and he loves to cook.

With the world in your hands and the Universe on your side, right now you have the power to transform yourself and your relationships.

Now you can see yourself as the love that you are.

Now you can let go of the past and begin again. Now you are in control of your destiny.

And *now* is the time to create your grand story.

The Committed Man is waiting...

Notes for the Love Addict

HOW TO SPOT A COMMITMENT PHOBE

The Chase: He loves the thrill of the chase, so beware of the big red flag when this guy is infatuated much too soon. His early desperate cries of love are an imbalance of emotion and irrational response. The minute you give him your love in return, he vanishes.

The Distant Servant: In the *beginning*, the Commitment Phobe would do anything for you, including washing your car or bringing you breakfast in bed. All the while, he remains elusively distant and a bit mysterious.

The Past: The Commitment Phobe hasn't had a serious relationship lasting over two years unless he was a very successful cheater. And he usually has a backup woman or two waiting in the wings.

Flowers: This charmer loves the idea of romance and will gladly adorn you with your favorite tulips!

Love Notes: One of the Commitment Phobe's favorite pastimes is writing little love notes. He does this because he truly wants to win you over.

Extracurricular Activities: This guy usually hides behind addiction, computers, games, sports, work and often other women.

The Fight: The Commitment Phobe will generally blame you for all of the relationship woes. He loves a good fight because it gives him more reason to leave. But when the relationship is going great, he panics.

The Cold Shoulder: This wolf in sheep's clothing suddenly, and without warning, becomes cold and distant. The love notes and flowers become a faint memory, and you want the man from the *beginning* back. But remember, the guy you first met was the wolf, not the sheep.

Sex Drive: Your once amazing sex life has suddenly dwindled into nothing. He no longer has any interest in the physical aspects of the relationship. This is because he knows he is leaving and cannot stomach the guilt of leading you on, or he has someone else on the side.

AND THE OSCAR GOES TO...

"I think I can see us together at some point in the future." The Commitment Phobe knows you like hearing that there is hope down the road without actually committing. He manipulates words to his advantage. In actuality, "future" means "later tonight."

"My ex was a crazy bitch." This is the Commitment Phobe's way of pointing out that he likes you better. Perfect, right? Not really. He is simultaneously deflecting responsibility for the downfall of his last relationship.

"I love hanging out with you, but I understand if you have to move on." The conscious Commitment Phobe is hoping he can get in a few more rounds of lovemaking while you think it out. Hey, at least he's being honest!

SIGNS OF A COMMITMENT PHOBE

1. Always looking around the corner for the better option.

2. Avoids labeling the relationship as much as possible.

3. Trouble dealing with feelings from the past.

4. Living two different lives.

5. Difficulty keeping his word and integrity.

6. Desperately wanting to find the perfect woman.

7. Always wanting to fit in.

8. Anxiety about having made the wrong choices or difficulty with upcoming decisions.

9. Difficult time trusting himself, often feeling he has no control.

10. Getting bored after the Honeymoon Phase and taking that as a signal to escape from the relationship.

SIGNS OF A LOVE ADDICT

1. Fear of being single.

2. Worried about what others think.

3. Manipulating/lying for love and attention.

4. Feeling a sense of abandonment from relationships and friendships.

5. Terrified of rejection.

6. Seeking to be "above" or "better than" others.

7. Tolerating abusive behavior.

8. Taking the blame just to diffuse conflict.

9. Scared of saying or doing the wrong thing.

10. Constantly analyzing her relationship.

FIVE QUESTIONS FOR THE LOVE ADDICT

While in a relationship, the Love Addict may begin to think that certain obsessive thoughts and feelings are normal. While her intentions are clear, her thinking is off. Ask yourself these five questions to get a better idea of whether or not you are addicted to love or involved with a Commitment Phobe.

1. Are you bombarded by thoughts of him leaving you for someone else?

2. Do you fantasize about seeing him hurt over losing you?

3. Do thoughts of him sexually involved with another woman make you physically ill?

4. Do you obsess over your looks and what others might say and think about you?

5. Do you worry you will never find a man as wonderful as the Commitment Phobe?

If you answered YES to all five questions, you could be a Love Addict. This is a strong indicator that you are thinking with fear rather than love. You likely do not truly love the Commitment Phobe, but rather you are drawn to him like a moth to a flame, confusing love for lust. Loving someone who treats you poorly is only a sign that you lack self-love.

HE'S NOT A JERK.
HE'S A COMMITMENT PHOBE.

I love men. All men. And I can spot a Commitment Phobe from miles away. But this does not mean they are not my friends, my family, my neighbors or my colleagues. Regardless of how it may seem, it may come as a surprise that I do not think the Commitment Phobe is an evil guy. This man has issues of his own...don't get me wrong. And I strongly believe that staying with a Commitment Phobe out of pity for his inner struggles is a recipe for unhappiness, especially when his struggles are pointed directly at you! Having compassion for him is one thing, but taking his issues on as a second job with little to no pay can be a real dead end.

DECIDING TO STAY

The Commitment Phobe can suffer a serious wake-up call if a Love Addict abandons him. In fact, it is usually the only wake-up call for a Commitment Phobe. He may come back genuinely willing to change. But buyer, beware: when the Commitment Phobe reenters the push/pull relationship, he always comes with promises. Keeping them and living them is another story. Some women will decide to stay in the relationship when tough love has paid off.

If the Love Addict and the Commitment Phobe are equally dedicated to resolving their own personal issues of abandonment and intimacy and want to support each other on the journey toward recovery, then there is hope for them. This may surprise you, as up until this point, I have been very adamant about the Commitment Phobe's stubborn demeanor and repeated relationship failures. A conscious Commitment Phobe who is open and willing to change can become a happier and more loving partner. But the truth remains that these cases are rare. The Commitment Phobe is just as deserving of love and just as valuable as anyone else, but he has to come to this realization.

Like all fears, commitment phobia is a wall to hide behind, and for the men who suffer from it, the lifelong effects can be debilitating. Realizing that there is nothing to fear but fear itself can be an eye-opening tour de force for the Commitment Phobe. But the Love Addict mustn't become his mother and persuade, coddle and stroke him into changing. Our job is to work on us, and his job is to work on him, supporting, not coercing each other. Continuing to sacrifice our own emotional and spiritual well-being will not help this relationship in the long run. When one changes, the other can follow. But when the Love Addict refuses to give up on the Commitment Phobe, and he is willing to do what is necessary for a healthy relationship, there are some important steps needed for success.

While working through the relationship with a Commitment Phobe, the Love Addict needs to be careful that she is still not influenced by his moods, making her vulnerable and still subject to his behaviors. The Love Addict has to get her own life together, with or without the Commitment Phobe. No one should be held to a higher importance over you.

We cannot emotionally and spiritually afford to stand by a man who is perpetually on the fence about whether or not he wants to marry us. Unless he has an awareness of his issues and a willingness to help himself, we should take a different path. If the Love Addict is insistent on keeping the Commitment Phobe around, there are things she can do in the interim:

1. **Forgive each other.**
Pay attention to the pattern, and move into forgiveness. Both parties may have relapses, and this is to be expected.

2. **Take continuous inventory of your own feelings.**
When either party is pushing or pulling, get in touch with the fear you feel and question where it comes from. Sit with that feeling and make a connection to it.

3. **Keep the lines of communication open.**
Speak clearly with each other about insecurities, childhood issues and unrealistic emotional needs. If both parties are willing to change and are open to helping themselves, be there for each other. Steer clear of telling him what he should be doing and keep the focus on your own growth.

4. **Be patient.**
Don't rush the natural progression of uncovering your past and confronting the truth. Each

party needs to go at his or her own pace, realizing this is a process.

5. Take responsibility.
You are only responsible for your own feelings, not your partner's. Drawing this clear line will keep you focused on cleaning up your own side of the street. If the Commitment Phobe promises to work on himself and weeks later has taken no serious action, know when to walk away.

Acknowledgements

My deepest gratitude goes out to my husband for allowing me the time and space to write this book and offer hope to Love Addicts everywhere.

Most of all, thank you to my friends and clients who were brave enough to come out from the shadows and be vulnerable and honest, confirming that love addiction needs to be talked about on a grander scale. Without these worthy souls, validating the truth about commitment phobia would have been impossible.

About the Author

Emily Wilcox is an author and relationship expert dedicated to helping women uncover the truth about love addiction. Having worked for many years to expose the reasons behind this push/pull relationship, she wanted to share her discovery with readers everywhere. After using the Law of Attraction and vowing never to attract another Commitment Phobe, Emily met her husband when she bumped into him on a crowded sidewalk in 2006.

Emily continues to coach individuals and couples on love addiction, commitment phobia, self-esteem, loss and the art of conscious relationships. She is the author of *100 Lesbians Walk Into a Bar*. She resides in Los Angeles, California.

www.thecommitmentphobe.com

References

Bach, R. (1973). *Jonathan Livingston Seagull: A Story.* New York, NY: Avon.

Brown, C. B. (2010). *The Gifts of Imperfection: Let Go of Who You Think You're Supposed to Be and embrace who you are.* Center City, MN: Hazelden.

Carter, S. & Sokol, J. (1983). *Men Who Can't Love: How to Recognize a Commitment Phobic Man Before He Breaks Your Heart.* New York, NY: Berkley Books.

Chopra, D. (1996). *The Way of the Wizard: Twenty Spiritual Lessons in Creating the Life You Want.* New York, NY: Harmony Books.

Chopra, D. (2005). *The Book of Secrets: Unlocking the Hidden Dimensions of Your Life.* New York, NY: Harmony Books.

Chopra, D. (2009). *The Ultimate Happiness Prescription: 7 Keys to Joy and Enlightenment.* New York, NY: Harmony Books.

Cohen, C. B. (2016). *Shots of Wit: A Collection of Original Aphorisms and Witticisms for Life.* Seattle, WA: Clifford B. Cohen.

Dass, R. (n.d.). *Ram Dass Quotes*. Retrieved from
https://www.ramdass.org/ram-dass-quotes/

Dyer, W. W. (n.d.). *Success Secrets* [Web log post].
Retrieved from https://www.drwaynedyer.
com/blog/success-secrets/

Dyer, W. W. (n.d.). *Goodreads Wayne W. Dyer
quotes.* Retrieved from https://www.goodreads.
com/author/quotes/2960.Wayne_W_Dyer

Emerson, R. W. (1841) *Prudence. In Essays: First
Series.* (n.p.).

Garfinkel, P. (2008, March 28). *Four noble
Buddha quotes* [Web log post]. Retrieved
from https://www.huffpost.com/entry/four-
noble-buddha-quotes_b_86728

Gawain, S. (2011). *Living in the Light: Follow Your
Inner Guidance to Create a New Life and a
New World.* Novato, CA: New World Library.

Gawain, S. (2016). *Creative Visualization: Use the
Power of Imagination to Create What You
Want in Your Life.* Novato, CA: New World
Library.

Gilbert, E. (2010). *Committed: A Skeptic Makes
Peace with Marriage.* New York, NY: Viking.

Gilbert, E. (2006). *Eat Pray Love: One Woman's
Search for Everything Across Italy, India, and
Indonesia.* New York, NY: Viking.

Graber, C. (2010, May 5). Happiness is a walk in the park. 60-Second Science [Podcast]. *Scientific American*. Retrieved from https://www.scientificamerican.com/podcast/episode/happiness-is-a-walk-in-the-park-10-05-05/

Gray, J. (1992). *Men are from Mars, Women are from Venus.* New York, NY: HarperCollins.

Katie, B. (2003). *Loving What Is: Four Questions that can Change Your Life.* New York, NY: Three Rivers Press.

Mellody, P. (2003). *Facing Love Addiction: Giving Yourself the Power to Change the Way You Love.* San Francisco, CA: HarperOne.

Mims, C. (2012, January 3). Study suggests health, not wealth, determines happiness. *ZDNet*. Retrieved from https://www.zdnet.com/article/study-suggests-health-not-wealth-determines-happiness/

Pirisi, A. (2017, April 12). Yogis score high on happiness. *Yoga Journal*. Retrieved from https://www.yogajournal.com/lifestyle/yogis-score-high-on-happiness

Sophocles. (n.d.). *Sophocles quotes*. Retrieved from https://www.brainyquote.com/quotes/sophocles_132846

Tolle, E. (2008) A New Earth: Awakening to Your Life's Purpose. New York, NY: Penguin.

Williamson, M. (1996). *A Return to Love: Reflections on the Principles of "A Course in Miracles."* San Francisco, CA: HarperOne.

Williamson, M. (2001). *Enchanted Love: The Mystical Power of Intimate Relationships.* New York: Simon & Schuster.

Williamson, M. (2012, January 22). Interview by K. Page [Web log post]. An interview with Marianne Williamson, Finding Love, *Psychology Today*. Retrieved from https://www.psychologytoday.com/us/blog/finding-love/201201/interview-marianne-williamson

Winfrey, O. (2019). *The Path Made Clear: Discovering Your Life's Direction and Purpose.* New York, NY: Flatiron Books.

Winfrey, O. (n.d.). *Goodreads Oprah Winfrey quotes*. Retrieved from https://www.goodreads.com/author/quotes/3518.Oprah_Winfrey

CPSIA information can be obtained
at www.ICGtesting.com
Printed in the USA
LVHW040556100320
649438LV00005B/252

9 781942